Observing
Primary Literacy

Margaret Perkins

Education at SAGE

SAGE is a leading international publisher of journals, books, and electronic media for academic, educational, and professional markets.

Our education publishing includes:

- accessible and comprehensive texts for aspiring education professionals and practitioners looking to further their careers through continuing professional development

- inspirational advice and guidance for the classroom

- authoritative state of the art reference from the leading authors in the field

Find out more at: **www.sagepub.co.uk/education**

Observing
Primary Literacy
Margaret Perkins

Los Angeles | London | New Delhi
Singapore | Washington DC

SAGE Publications Ltd
1 Oliver's Yard
55 City Road
London EC1Y 1SP

SAGE Publications Inc.
2455 Teller Road
Thousand Oaks, California 91320

SAGE Publications India Pvt Ltd
B 1/I 1 Mohan Cooperative Industrial Area
Mathura Road
New Delhi 110 044

SAGE Publications Asia-Pacific Pte Ltd
33 Pekin Street #02–01
Far East Square
Singapore 048763

Library of Congress Control Number: 2011928828

British Library Cataloguing in Publication data

A catalogue record for this book is available from the British
Library

ISBN 978-0-85702-158-8
ISBN 978-0-85702-159-5 (pbk)

Typeset by Dorwyn, Wells, Somerset
Printed in Great Britain by CPI Group (UK) Ltd,
Croydon, CRO 4YY
Printed on paper from sustainable resources

MIX
Paper from
responsible sources
FSC
www.fsc.org   FSC® C013604

For Jonathan, Hannah and Ben

CONTENTS

ABOUT THE AUTHOR

Margaret Perkins has been working in initial teacher education for many years with undergraduates, postgraduates and those on employment-based routes in different provider institutions. She is an experienced primary teacher and has gone back into school to teach for periods varying between a day and a year since entering higher education. For the last six years, she has been responsible for the primary Graduate Teacher Programme at the University of Reading. This is a large programme which works with trainees in schools located in more than eight different authorities. It is this experience which prompted the writing of this book.

ACKNOWLEDGEMENTS

This book would not have been possible without all those teachers and trainee teachers who have shared their teaching with me. I am so grateful to them for allowing me to visit and observe them, to take away their plans and work, to talk with them about teaching and to intrude into their over-busy working lives. Thank you to them all. They are: Jonathan Nice, Helen Canham, Mark Dodds, Debbie Elsdon, Jo Yates, Carly Trillow, Jane Gow, Lisa Wallage, Alison Pumfrey, Chris Palmer, Vanessa Wilcher, Clare Castle, Tamalia Reeves, Lorna Anderton, Catherine Rodrigues, Paula Jenkins, Charlotte Wissett, Amy Smith, Chris Palmer, Zara Hoddle and Chrissie Brookes. I apologise to anyone who feels I have misrepresented their work and to anyone whose work I have inadvertently used without acknowledgement. Please contact me and I will put it right. Any fault is mine entirely.

I would also like to thank my friend and colleague, Prue Goodwin. She gave me her time by talking through ideas, reading drafts and continually reminding me of what lies at the heart of literacy.

Finally, thank you to Jesus for everything.

INTRODUCTION: OBSERVATION AND REFLECTION

There are so many books about teaching literacy in the primary school that it seems sensible to begin by stating what this book is not:

- It is not a book which aims to tell you how to teach literacy.
- It is not a book about current policies on teaching literacy (whenever you happen to be reading it and whatever the current policy may be).
- It does not cover everything that might be described as primary literacy.
- It does not only give examples of excellent practice.

You may now be wondering why you should bother reading this book at all! It is aimed at those who are training to be primary teachers and those who have just begun to be primary teachers. However, those who have been teaching for a while may still find something useful in it. Look at the title – *Observing Primary Literacy*. That is what this book is about.

During a training programme most trainee teachers will encounter teachers who have expertise in literacy and often have a passion for the subject. They will tell trainees about good practice, will inform them of the theoretical underpinning and give trainees many practical ideas for putting that into practice. I know that is what happens because it is what I do myself most days! Tutors will then tell trainees to go into schools and observe all these wonderful things happening. That is where the problem starts. Trainees go into schools and see lots of wonderful things but they are not the exact same wonderful things their tutors were talking about. The result is that either trainees stop observing, thinking that the teachers are hopelessly out of date, or they stop observing, thinking that their tutors are hopelessly out of touch.

In this book I hope to resolve that dilemma by turning things on their head. Instead of starting with the theory and giving examples of what it looks like in practice, I have started with what is going on in schools and considered how that relates to current understandings. My hope is that this will help trainee teachers to make their own observations more profitable. There are several consequences to this approach:

- The observations are messy. They are real – I collected them in real class-rooms over many years. I did not ask teachers to do anything special – I just watched and recorded what they did. In this way, I hoped to be like a trainee teacher sent into school to observe. I did not always know what I was going to see before I saw it.
- The observations are not examples of exemplary teaching. Some of the observations are of trainee teachers and some are of Advanced Skills Teachers. Nobody put on a special performance because I was there. Some of the lessons were rather mundane and others were exciting. Some worked well and others not so well. I think they reflect everyday classroom practice. Nothing was written or done especially for this book.
- The observations do not cover every aspect of literacy teaching and learn-ing. I think that most of the important things are covered in this book but not in as much detail as could be. That is not the purpose of this book. I hope this book will model to you how to observe in schools and what to do with your observations.

Observation

When training to teach, a lot of emphasis is put on observing experienced teachers. This is where teacher training is not like other learning experiences. When learning to drive you were not taken to the side of the road and told to watch experienced drivers; when learning to swim you did not sit at the side and watch good swimmers go up and down the pool. However, it is claimed that observation is a valuable way of learning how to be a teacher.

The problem is that good teaching is invisible; it is like a swan who glides beautifully along the river while, unseen to the observer, there is frantic activity going on underneath the surface. Teaching is just like that. Often, when sitting in the corner of a classroom, observing an experienced teacher, it can all seem so easy. That is because you are only seeing the surface and all the activity cannot be seen on the surface. This book gives you a snorkel and goggles and helps you to go beneath the surface and know what it is that supports the visible teaching.

Secondly, this book will help you to make your observations more purposeful by showing you what is important to look at and what can be overlooked. It is easy to be so busy looking at one thing that a key event is taking place which you miss.

Thirdly, this book helps you to see classroom activity with fresh eyes. Most trainee teachers have spent some time in schools before starting their training and are familiar with day-to-day classroom life. There is much that becomes taken for granted. This will help you to 'make the familiar strange.'

Finally, this book will help you to ask questions about what is seen. It cannot and does not purport to give all the answers, but it does ask lots of questions, and in asking questions, I would argue, we are often guided towards a deeper understanding. Many very experienced teachers operate at the intuitive level and find articulating reasons for their practice either very difficult or very challenging. I hope that this book will help trainees make their own meaning from classroom life by the questions they ask and the connections they make. It could almost be said that the observations are the text and trainees are being guided towards making their own meaning from them with the support of the commentary in the book.

In this introduction I focus on three aspects which all relate to the key purpose of the book, which is to help you make sense of classroom observations. There is a section about learning, about observing and about being a teacher.

About learning

How do you learn best? I learn best by writing. If I need to remember something or make sense of a difficult idea, I write, covering pages and pages with notes that afterwards make little sense to me. It is the process of committing thoughts and words to paper that helps me learn. My daughter also learns by writing, but her writing is neat and orderly and she refers to it again and again. She makes mind maps and PowerPoint presentations and will return to them many times. At the end, she has a valuable resource of notes and thoughts. My son learns best by talking. If he has to learn or revise something, he will sit and explain it to me, or whoever else happens to be around. He will ask for opinions and ideas, and will discuss and argue for hours. At the end there will be no visible final product but he will have made sense of it for himself and will 'know' what he needs to know.

What do these different ways of learning have in common? In our own way, we are making the body of knowledge, the concept or the skill our own. We are taking it and 'playing' with it until it is familiar and part of our understanding. This is what learning is about. We have not really learned something if it is just stuck onto the edge of our thinking, it needs to be assimilated until it is an integral part of our conceptual framework. Moon expresses this in a more 'academic' way: 'The process of learning is not … about the accumulation of material of learning, but about the process of changing conceptions' (2004: 17).

Learning to be a teacher happens in much the same way. At the beginning we try to emulate behaviours and language that we see, but it never really works. All trainee teachers lament the fact that an experienced teacher will walk into the classroom and the children will be quiet, but when the trainee walks in and, on the surface, does exactly the same thing, nothing happens. We can learn a long list of behaviour management strategies; we can know how to ask open questions and open up dialogue; we can be adept at organising and managing the class but it is only when we *become* a teacher, rather than just acting like one, that we really understand the social and intellectual framework of the classroom and can make professional judgements of our own.

If we are to learn in this way we need to explore what we see and dig deep below the surface. I hope that this book will help you to do that. What we learn needs to be close to our current understanding before we take the next small step in understanding. Two trainees might watch the same lesson and they will each learn something different. That is to be expected. We need to ensure, however, that our understanding changes. If our observations just confirm what we already know and do not lead us to question or challenge our current position, we will not learn.

> **Read**
> Moon, J.E. (2004) *A Handbook of Reflective and Experiential Learning: Theory and Practice.* Abingdon: RoutledgeFalmer.

What it is important to remember about learning before we begin to observe:

- Before we begin we need to be sure what we already know.
- Learning begins by asking questions.

- Everybody learns in a different way.
- We have not really learned something until it is a part of us.

About observing

Often we think it is easy to observe and so do not give much thought to it. We walk into a classroom, notebook and pencil ready, sit in the corner and write down everything that happens. It will not be long, however, before we realise that it is not that simple. When do we start recording and when do we end? Do we record everything? Can we join in while we are observing?

There are several principles of observation which, if remembered and observed, will help your observations to be more useful to you:

- *Focus.* Before beginning an observation, decide what you are looking at. If you want to learn about teachers' questioning skills, then just note all the events happening concerning questions. You do not need to record everything in the classroom. If you want to observe a teacher's behaviour management strategies then you need to record what he does when he uses them; you do not need to write down everything that happens all through the lesson. Be clear about the focus and purpose of your observation.
- *Expectations of the lesson.* It is always helpful to talk with the teacher before you observe a lesson, so that you know what the purpose of the lesson is and what the teacher hopes to achieve. If possible ask the teacher for a copy of the plans; this will help you both to plan your observation and also to be aware of what the lesson is about.
- *Record objectively.* It is important to record exactly what you see and hear and be careful not to make an instant interpretation. Note the difference between this observation:
  J was bored with the lesson and kept looking around to see what other children were doing
  and this one:
  J wriggled while sitting on the carpet. He turned around six times during the input and looked at the children immediately behind him.
  You will see that the second observation states what J did but the first one puts an interpretation on those actions. You have no way of knowing that J was bored; you have just seen what he did.
- *Reflect on what you have observed.* Earlier in the chapter I said that learning comes from asking questions of what is known so that our current understanding is challenged. After an observation it is important to read through your observations carefully and look for anything that surprises you and is unexpected. Match what you have seen against what you have known, and

note those things which contradict your expectations.

- *Ask questions.* Having noticed the unusual and unexpected, ask questions. Why was J wriggling? Was it because the floor was hard? Was he bored? Did he want to go to the toilet? Was somebody behind surreptitiously poking him? Look beneath the surface. Why did the teacher ask that question to that particular child? Why did that child respond in that way?
- *Draw conclusions.* At the end of every observation ask yourself the question, 'What have I learned?' Remember what your focus was and articulate what you have learned about that focus. How did you learn that? Can you explain your learning to somebody else? How has your understanding of that issue developed?
- *Plan future learning.* What do you need to do next? Do you need to read something to explain what you have observed? Do you need to do another observation to check it out? Do you need to ask the teacher or the children to explain something to you?

About becoming a teacher

Becoming a teacher is about becoming a professional, and that means making decisions and judgements about children and pedagogy. In order to make an informed decision, it is necessary to understand why teachers do what they do and why they choose not to do certain things. This means you need to reflect on what you have observed. What does it mean to reflect?

Schön (1983) defined reflective practice as, 'the capacity to reflect on action so as to engage in a process of continuous learning'. Teachers are continually making decisions based on what is happening in the classroom and Schön argues that this 'reflection-in-action' leads to professional knowledge gained from experience which informs that decision-making. Observing other teachers gives the trainee teachers the chance to step back and reflect on what is happening in classrooms. This can sometimes be challenging. In the immediacy of classroom activity, it can be difficult for even very experienced teachers to fully appreciate what is going on. I showed one teacher, whom I observed for the book, my comments on her lesson and her response was, 'I did not know all that was happening'.

The term 'observation' is used in the broadest sense. The observations in the book contain all those things that, in my experience, trainee teachers are asked to look at and learn from:

- lessons being taught
- lesson plans
- unit of work plans

- children's work
- conversations about practice.

How the book works

Observations, in whatever form they take, are presented in detail. A running commentary is provided which explains what is happening, relates it to theory and asks questions to help you to reflect. As each chapter progresses the commentary becomes thinner and the questions increase. The book is designed to provide a model and a scaffold for trainee teachers as they go into schools to observe. The importance of school-based training is increasing and it seems likely that more and more training will take place in schools (White Paper, *The Importance of Teaching*, DfE 2010). This makes it increasingly important that trainee teachers know how to make sense of what they see and are able to ask questions of it. In this way they will become critically reflective practitioners able to respond professionally to the demands placed upon them as teachers.

CHAPTER 1

UNDERSTANDING TEXTS

Texts are at the heart of literacy. All the observations in this chapter explore what counts as a text in literacy teaching and learning, teachers' knowledge of texts and the place of texts within the school and classroom.

The Office for Standards in Education, Children's Services and Skills (Ofsted) report *Reading by Six: How the Best Schools Do It* (2010) has at its heart the belief that learning to read is the most important thing that schools can teach children and looks at 12 schools which are deemed to be successful in this. The summary of findings and recommendations attributes the success of these schools to 'a very rigorous and sequential approach … through systematic phonics.' (Ofsted 2010: 4) This is clearly very important and in Chapter 3 we consider some observations of strategies for teaching reading, including phonics. However, it is interesting that Ofsted makes no mention in the summary of findings and recommendations of what children read, and it is that which is the focus of this first chapter. I have deliberately called the first chapter 'Understanding texts' because it seems to me essential as teachers to consider how the texts we use impact on children learning to be both readers and writers.

If I reflect on my own behaviour as a reader, I know that *what* I read greatly affects *how* I read. There are some novels which I read really quickly, skimming over descriptive passages because I only want to know what happens, yet I have just finished rereading Jane Austen's *Persuasion* and I read that really slowly, savouring in the delights of Austen's language. If I am reading a magazine, I skim over the text to get the gist of the subject matter but, if I am reading an academic textbook or article, I will read slowly, frequently rereading sections and sometimes reading aloud to make sure I truly understand. Think about your own reading behaviour and note how the text you are reading affects how you read.

My knowledge of texts also affects how I write. In writing this, I am imagining I am talking to my current group of students. I have particular faces in mind and am remembering how they respond in lectures. I am also remembering other textbooks I have read for trainee teachers and am recalling their style and 'voice' as I write. Earlier today I wrote a reference for somebody and wrote in a very different style; I used a set format and thought carefully about how each word would be interpreted. I have also been working on an article for an academic journal and before writing looked at several past editions of the journal, reading other articles to see the style of writing that was acceptable. This emphasises again, the centrality of the text in the processes of reading and writing.

What counts as a text?

It will be clear from the previous two paragraphs that I read and write a variety of texts and there are even more which are an integral part of my daily life. Just this morning I have read and written emails, updated my status on a social network site and read the statuses of friends, looked for information on lots of different Internet sites, read the post and yesterday's newspaper, checked my diary and written in two new appointments, written notes on sticky pads as I took phone calls, read and sent texts on my mobile phone, looked on a spreadsheet to find information for the accountant and checked the label on the yoghurt for the sell-by date. All that happened in the space of 4 hours. The texts I read and wrote were all very different in their purposes, formats and audiences. My teenage children read and create an even greater range of texts using, among other things, pencils, keyboards, visual images, sound, photographs and film.

What is common about all these different kinds of texts is that in both reading and creating them the communication of meaning lies at the heart of all that is done. Texts may use a variety of methods or modes to convey or express meaning – words, pictures, images, photographs, video clips, sound files, hyperlinks. Some texts use several of these and they are known as multi-modal texts. Reading and creating a multi-modal text requires many more skills than reading or writing written texts and children in the twenty-first century need to be skilled in all these modes of communication. The knowledge required to be an effective reader and writer today is very different from when I learned a long time ago and I am often conscious that I am catching up in my skill base.

Whatever the nature of a text, what we are reading or creating matters and it is through encounters with texts that children learn what it is to be a reader and writer. Over 20 years ago Margaret Meek wrote a very influential book about this very thing, and in more recent times Vivienne Smith has written about why texts matter in the way in which children become readers.

Read

Meek, M. (1988) *How Texts Teach What Readers Learn*. Stroud: Thimble Press.
Smith, V. (2008) 'Learning to be a reader: promoting good textual health' in P. Goodwin (ed.), *Understanding Children's Books: A Guide for Education Professionals*. London: Sage.

Reflect

How does what Meek and Smith say relate to multi-modal texts?

The observations in this chapter put texts at the centre of teaching primary literacy and the first observation concerns a unit of work where the study of texts informed children's creation of their own texts.

OBSERVATION: The first two lessons of a Year 4 (ages 8 and 9) class unit of work with an author focus

This unit of work formed part of cross-curricular work in Design and Technology, Art and Literacy. The intention of the whole unit was for the children in the class to make their own books, hopefully inspired by a visit from the author, Paul Gerhaghty. He is a South African, now living in London, who writes and illustrates children's books. The illustrations capture the light of Africa with its vibrant colours; they are bright and yet soft and full of curves. The stories are a strange mix of reality and anthromorphism – they explore human values, relationships and emotions but within the context of real animal behaviour. Many of the stories are based on observed real-life incidents from Africa.

The first lesson of the unit took place on the morning of the author's visit. There were two learning objectives:

- to be able to evaluate the work of an author
- to understand the relationship between text and images in a picture book.

The lesson began with an introduction to Paul Gerhaghty, giving a taster of information about him and informing the children that he was going to come and talk to them that afternoon. That generated a lot of excitement among the children.

Comment

It could be argued that the children were not given much notice of the author visit and there was limited time for preparation. The teacher would argue that the immediacy of the visit gave a sense of urgency to the lesson and the children were highly motivated and engaged. What do you think?

The teacher then read the book *Over the Steamy Swamp* to the class using a visualiser so that they could see the illustrations. This is a story bringing the food chain to life. A mosquito flies over a swamp; behind her hovers a dragonfly; behind her sits a frog; and so it continues. The strong illustrations are colourful and there is a humour to the whole text. After the reading the children were asked to talk with their partners and share first impressions of the book.

Comment

Notice how the teacher first asks the children to make a personal response to the book. It is really important that children are given the opportunity to do this before they begin any more detailed analysis of the text. Michael Rosen says: 'We read because it either gives us pleasure or because there is something we want to know. In other words, we read for the meaning.' (2010: 2)

Note also that the children are asked to talk about their responses with their partners. We will see over and over again how important talk is in the learning process. It helps to clarify ideas, to extend understanding and develop thinking by engaging in debate.

An extremely useful framework for this has been established by Aiden Chambers. He suggests the following three 'sharings' as we talk about books we have read:

Enthusiasms – what is it that excites you about the book? These enthusiasms can be either positive or negative and can relate to plot, setting, character, style or anything at all.

Puzzles – what questions do you have about the book? What is it you don't understand? Are there any gaps for you? Where do you want to go 'behind the scenes?

Patterns – what patterns or links do you notice as you read the book? Are there patterns in the language used, in the illustrations, in recurring elements of the plot, in characters' behaviours or in links to other texts you have read or to real-life experiences?

I have used this framework with children from age 3 upwards, with students and with my peers when discussing books we have read. **Read** more about it and the importance of giving children time to talk about books in:

Chambers, A. (2011) *Tell Me (Children, Reading and Talk) with The Reading Environment.* Stroud: Thimble Press.

You might also want to look at the work Pie Corbett has done on 'Booktalk' which will give practical ideas of how to implement Chambers' approach.

After the pair talk the class were asked to get into their well-established literacy groups to evaluate the book. First, as a class they discussed what it meant to evaluate a book and what they needed to look for when reading. Their discussion yielded a list which included such questions as:

- Is the story exciting?
- Is it funny?
- Is the language good? Does it help me to make pictures in my mind?
- Do the illustrations add anything to the words? Do they tell a different story?
- Do the characters seem real? Can we believe what they say and do?
- What are the best and worst bits?
- Would I recommend this book to a friend?

> **Comment**
>
> The questions generated by this class would indicate that they have had a lot of experience in talking about and evaluating texts. A class is unlikely to come up with such questions without these experiences. Consider how this helps the children develop their reading skills and behaviour as readers.

The children then worked in their groups. Each group produced a written evaluation of the text. They worked together; one child was elected as scribe. The groups were of mixed ability and so those less confident in writing were able to make as much contribution as others without the pressure of having to write all their thoughts down.

> **Comment**
>
> It is important to remember that because a child struggles with recording ideas this does not mean that the ideas are not as powerful as those of other children. This teacher used mixed ability groups with a more able child as scribe. What other strategies can you think of?

The children were given just 20 minutes to complete their evaluations. They were written in note form and were not particularly neat! In this instance that did not matter because the purpose of the writing was to record discussion in order to remember. This was writing used for an authentic purpose.

At the end of the lesson the class came together and shared key points. The teacher recorded these and ensured the children were able to give concrete examples from the text for each point that was made. There then followed a short discussion on any questions or comments the children might want to put to Paul Geraghty in the afternoon.

> **Reflect**
>
> How well prepared do you think the children were for the author visit? What knowledge and understanding had the morning's lesson given them?

Paul Geraghty visited in the afternoon and this further stimulated the children's interest in his work. Among other things he talked about how some ideas became books and how some did not! He showed actual examples of idea doodle-sheets, presentation thumbnails (a kind of cartoon-strip miniature of the story used to show to editors), rough drawings, finished illustrations, proof prints, the book as a large running sheet – prior to cutting – bound proofs and, finally, the finished book, which was then read to the group, who then asked questions.

The next day the children began to plan their own books. The lesson began by looking at the structure and characteristics of a story. The teacher started by asking the children to remember stories they had particularly enjoyed and to tell their partners a simple outline of the plot. The class then came back together and the teacher showed them the story hill pro forma.

Comment

This activity worked for several reasons. First, it began with the children's own experiences; they were talking about books they knew well and so were confident enough to share ideas. Secondly, they were telling the story to one other person; this gave them confidence to 'have a go' as mistakes would be relatively private. Thirdly, the 'theory' came out of the children's analysis and discussion of well-known stories and so they were able to make it their own. Deep learning is not about repeating what you have been told, it is about transforming knowledge into personal understanding.

All stories have basically the same structure:

opening → build up → climax/conflict → resolution → ending

Many resources are available to help with this, and the story hill is just one of them. It can be found on www.primaryresources.co.uk. Another idea is to take each part of a story and match it to one finger on your hand; you can then hold your story in your hand.

The teacher then read the class another Paul Geraghty book, *Solo*. This is about Solo the penguin chick who is left alone in the Antarctic when her mother leaves to search for food. The tension of the book comes from the uncertainty of Solo's survival.

The children shared their personal responses as before but this time focused more closely on the relationship between the illustrations and the written text. The teacher asked them to consider how Paul Geraghty had told the story through the different elements of the book. As a whole class they then matched the narrative of *Solo* to the story hill pro forma.

The children were then sent off to plan a story they were going to tell in the book they would make. They were given the options of brainstorming on their own, of talking about it with a friend or of drafting it out on the story hill. They could choose any or all of these strategies as long as they had firmly fixed in their minds the story they wanted to tell.

> **Comment**
>
> Note how the teacher allowed the children to choose how they planned their story. He offered them different ways of working, and in reality allowed other ways he had not offered. All he wanted was that, at the end of the allotted time, each child had the outline of a story in their head. He did not even worry if they had not written it down, as long as the children were sure they could remember it and were able to tell it to somebody else. Reflecting on your own learning will remind you that learners do best when they are allowed to work in the ways which suit them. For teachers it is important to keep focused on the learning objective and that will enable you to realise what is important and what is not.

There were several more lessons during that week in which the children worked on their story and each created their own book. They were then able to share their books with each other and eventually put them in the class library.

What can we learn from this observation?

- The first thing that needs to be said is that real texts are central to all the work. If we want children to be readers and writers they need to understand the purposes of reading and writing. By using real books as models for understanding and analysing what authors do to make a book successful, children come to understand what literacy is all about. Reading and talking about multilayered texts and listening to authors talk is a more powerful teaching strategy for effective writing than lots of exercises adding in 'wow' words and connectives to sentences.
- Secondly, this lesson reminds us that children learn in different ways and lessons need to cater for this and be flexible in the opportunities offered to children. Teachers need to be clear about the purpose of a lesson or a sequence of lessons and allow children the time to move towards it in the way which suits them best. One approach will not suit all children.
- Thirdly, working with texts means looking at every aspect of the text and not just decoding the printed word. The illustrations in Paul Geraghty's books contribute to the meaning of the whole – the style, colour, shapes and light all evoke atmosphere and help the reader to make sense of the story. The choice of words and the order in which they are written also matter. The size of the pages, the arrangement of words and pictures and

the font used, all contribute to the whole. As pupils talk about books they will come to understand this, and these children, as they created their books, were doing much more than just writing a story – they were composing a whole text.

Teachers choosing books

If teachers are going to make texts the centre of their literacy teaching, they need to have an extensive knowledge of children's texts themselves. If they are going to choose texts which will demonstrate to children the power of the written word, they need to have read, thought and talked about these texts. It is clear, therefore, that teachers need to have a strong knowledge of children's books. The Teachers as Readers project (Cremin, Bearne, Mottram and Goodwin 2007–10) looked at this very issue and one of the main aims of the project was to discover the extent of teachers' knowledge of children's literature. They found that this knowledge was 'severely limited'. The research team suggested that the requirement of the National Literacy Strategy to focus on 'significant authors' has limited the authors which teachers use in their teaching.

The teachers in the sample knew such a narrow range of authors that they were unlikely to be able to make recommendations to their pupils beyond the narrow range that teachers already used in their classroom. Most of the authors named by the teachers in the sample were extremely well known.

Read

Cremin, T., Mottram, M., Bearne, E. and Goodwin, P. (2008) 'Exploring teachers' knowledge of children's literature', *Cambridge Journal of Education*, 38(4) 449–64.

How extensive is your knowledge of children's books?

OBSERVATION: Talking to teachers about reading aloud to children

A few years ago a colleague and I (Goodwin and Perkins 2009, 2010) did some small-scale research on reading aloud to children. We did this because, although reading aloud to children is a definite expectation within the Literacy Framework, anecdotal evidence suggested that it was not happening frequently. Our underpinning belief was that reading aloud is much more than an enjoyable experience, although one hopes it is that, but is also an important lesson in any teaching of reading programme. We wanted to find out if teachers did read aloud to their classes, and the reasons they had for doing this if they did. We found that teachers did read aloud to their classes but saw it mainly as a good way to establish social cohesion in a class. It was not something which was planned and happened most often at the very end of the day. It tended not to feature in planning.

Reasons given for reading aloud included the introduction of different types of authors, books and texts to children. However, it seemed that the choice of texts read was mainly made by the children themselves, with teachers sometimes selecting their own favourite texts.

Comment
Can you see any contradiction in these statements?

There were no surprises in the types of texts read to children: short stories, poetry, picture books, comics and magazines, and a few others including newspapers, e-books, charts, song words, non-fiction and a joke book. Our sample named 220 books, including fiction texts, children's novels and single stories, collections of short stories (5), picture books (mostly younger readers), traditional tales (myths, folk tale, legend), five poetry books (2 classic poems) and three non-fiction (all in narrative form).

Comment
Imagine you are the teacher of a class in a particular year group. Can you list the key authors and/or texts you would want to be absolutely sure the children in your class encountered?

If we accept the view that the texts that children encounter are important in the learning process, as teachers we need to ensure we know the best texts to introduce them to. How can teachers do that? The Teachers as Researchers project (United Kingdom Literacy Association 2007–10) claims that teachers should be readers who model reading behaviours and create communities of readers. This means that they will provide children with time to get totally absorbed in a book, they will read aloud to them and offer books the children can read with ease. In order to do this, teachers need to be fully confident to make decisions about all the different texts used to teach literacy in their classrooms.

Finding your way through the hundreds if not thousands of children's books which are published and making an informed decision seems a daunting task unless you can turn to an expert for advice and support. Teachers urgently need librarians beside them when they set out to create confident young readers.

> The skills and knowledge offered by librarians have never been as necessary as they are now when successive governments have imposed a didactic reading curriculum and many teachers have lost confidence in their intuitive use of literature with their pupils. In education we need the support and positive input of librarians to reinvigorate the teaching of reading. (Goodwin 2011)

The role of libraries

Libraries have always provided access to the worlds of information and literature for everyone. Wherever I have worked, there has always been a public library from which to borrow books whether I have needed books for information, to learn something new or for the delight of a well-written tale. Most schools have a library – whether it be a purpose-built area with space for books, browsers and displays, or a few shelves in an old stock cupboard – a school with a library shows a commitment to literacy. There is little national support for teacher librarians in primary schools, which makes the School Library Association (SLA) well worth joining as it offers advice and support to anyone who organises a school library. Some (but increasingly fewer) local authorities fund a School Library Services (SLS) with centralised book collections and support staff. The SLS usually provides schools with collections of books to support learning. These days, most local SLS have to charge a fee for its service. However, several hundred pounds would be nothing compared with the thousands it would cost to buy the books – not to mention the advice. Public libraries also do their best to support schools with literacy learning. Baby Bounce and Rhyme Time, storytelling for the under 5s, Summer Reading Challenge events and book awards all invite children into the world of reading. It is unfortunate that teachers do not always make the most of these very valuable assets.

> **Read**
>
> Look at the website of the School Library Association and see what support they can offer you as a teacher (www.sla.org.uk).
>
> In particular download the Primary Schools Library Charter and use it to reflect on libraries in schools where you have observed. There is more about libraries in schools in Chapter 5.

Children's views on texts

Having considered the importance of teachers' understanding of texts, the next section looks at what children think about the texts they read. I talked to groups of children in Foundation Stage 2 (age 4–5) and Year 1 (age 5–6) and Year 2 (age 6–7) about their views of the books they read. I sat with groups of children in the school library and asked them to tell me about reading. It was not possible to record the conversations but I made detailed notes immediately afterwards.

OBSERVATION: Conversations with children

1. Reception children (ages 4 and 5)

All the children said that they liked reading and their choice of favourite book seemed to be either the book they were reading at present or had read recently, or something they had seen on the television or at the cinema. All the children said reading happened a lot at home; they read to their mums and their mums read to them. They talked about going to visit the local library with their mums to choose books. They enjoyed this time of reading; it happened on the sofa or in bed and was associated with cuddles and was a cosy social time. Reading at home was all about enjoying a text together.

In contrast, they described reading at school as 'work' and they identified those in the class who were 'good readers' as those who were good at decoding. Reading in school was a serious business and not to be taken lightly; one little boy said to me: 'If we read it quickly, we might be trying to get on to another book but that's not really learning.' All their comments on reading in school were dominated by the colour of the book they were reading. One child said, 'I was the first one in our group to be on green books'.

> **Comment**
> These children had been in school for only two terms and were already making a clear distinction between reading at home and reading at school. They talked about books at home in terms of what they were about and whether they liked them or not; they talked about books in school as to how high up the scheme they were.

2. Year 1 children (ages 5 and 6)

Again all these children said they liked reading. They had all brought their school reading book to the library with them and when I asked them what their favourite reading book was, every child chose that one. All of the children said they read at home but several said they only read school books at home to practise for reading at school. One boy told me that his mum had bought him a complete reading scheme so he could practise more at home. Reading at home was, as with the younger children, associated with a sociable comfortable time, on the sofa or in bed.

Every child knew which colour book they were on in school and, indeed, they all knew which colour book everybody in the class was on. I had no way of knowing if they were correct or not but there was a strong and confident consensus in the group!

Of the children who told me they were reading a different book at home, the books they described were significantly more challenging to read than the reading books from school they had with them; for example, one child said he was reading a book from the Horrible Histories series.

> **Comment**
> For these children, who in their reading experiences at school were beginning to decode independently, reading was measured by the success they had achieved in doing this. Reading in school was almost a competition and success was measured by how much was achieved. The children were not able to tell me what their school reading books were about, all that mattered to them about these books were their colour.

3. Year 2 children (ages 6 and 7)

Pleasure in reading was not unanimous among these children; some enjoyed reading but some did not. It tended to be that the girls said they enjoyed reading but the boys did not. When I probed deeper, however, the picture was slightly different. One boy said he only likes reading comics and magazines. He gave me a very detailed description of the magazines he read, which were all related to the Playstation 3. He told me he reads the magazines to find out about games and to help him decide which ones he wants to play. Another boy was adamant that he did not like reading at all. He went on to tell me that he supports Arsenal and every day reads the sport pages of the *Sun* newspaper. He explained to me how by doing this he can find out how Arsenal is doing and that by looking at the tables and reading the match reports he can work out if they are going to win their next game. He was describing some very sophisticated reading behaviour but according to the colour of the reading book he had been given in school he was not a very good reader.

Comment

A lot of work has been done on boys and reading, and the observations above are very limited and small examples of the issue. They raise some important points however. The boys who said they did not like reading and did not read, actually engaged in some very demanding reading. I do not know how much help they received at home but it was evident that this reading served a particular purpose related to the boys' interests.

The Ofsted report *English 2000–05: A Review of Inspection Survey* (2005: 32) said that, 'Boys tend to give up independent reading more easily than girls and, as they get older, seem to have greater difficulty in finding books to enjoy'. Lockwood (2008), in his research on reading for pleasure found that 77 per cent of boys claimed to like to read a book compared with 91 per cent of girls. Seventy-two per cent of boys enjoyed non-fiction compared with 57 per cent of girls. These patterns seem to be becoming established in these young children.

All the children in this Year 2 group said they did not read much at school and only read when the teacher told them to do so.

Comment

All the children clearly read a lot in school in the course of a day's activities but they did not recognise it as such unless they were reading from something which had been given the label 'reading book'. What are the implications of this for classroom practice?

The children also seemed to think that reading in school was all about decoding. They did not mention enjoyment of the books they read at all. They told me that there was supposed to be a story time at school when the teacher read to them just before they go home from school but usually it was a bit late and they missed it because they had not finished their work or were still getting changed from PE. One girl told me, 'In hard books there are more sounds which make up a word. You use up quite a lot of sounds and letters to make a word'.

Comment

The children in this school achieve highly in standard assessments and are very competent at one aspect of reading. A lot of emphasis is placed on the teaching of decoding through systematic phonics teaching and it is clearly successful. However, in one aspect of reading they are not so competent. As Dombey (2010: 5) said:

> 'A balanced approach means, that, as well as working to master the mechanics of reading that allows them to lift the words off the page, children are encouraged and supported to focus on making sense of written text, and to see its uses in ordering, enlarging, enjoying and making sense of their lives. It means ensuring that classrooms are filled with interesting written texts – on screen as well as on paper – and that children are given rich experiences of putting these texts to use.'

Read

Dombey, H. (2010) *Teaching Reading: What the Evidence Says*. Leicester: The United Kingdom Literacy Association.

Activity

Talk to children in a Year 5 or 6 class and see if they think differently from these Key Stage 1 children.

The attitudes reflected in the observations above pose an interesting challenge for literacy teachers and the next two observations pick up on Dombey's comment that classrooms should be full of interesting written texts. Before you read the observations, think what this means to you and consider what sort of texts you would want to put in your classroom.

The classroom as a reading environment

If teachers want to encourage children to read and write, it is important that they create classrooms which are stimulating literacy environments that offer time, space and resources for reading. What might such a classroom look like?

OBSERVATION: Looking at a Year 1 classroom

The classroom is colourful, light and airy. It is one-half of a very large room which is shared with the parallel class. The windows are large. There is a large book corner which has bookshelves on three sides of it and a Kinderbox (a box containing large picture books) as well. There is a rug on the floor and several large cushions. On the edge of the book corner there is an old armchair covered with a throw and filled with cushions. The teacher sits here for read-aloud sessions and children are frequently curled up here reading; it is known in the class as the 'story chair'.

On top of a unit just to the side of the book corner is a display entitled 'Our Book of the Week'. This week it is Mo Willems's book *Don't Let the Pigeon Drive the Bus*. There are several copies of the book here and children can read them at any time. There are also laminated copies of pages from the book with laminated speech bubbles, some blank and some containing the words from the text. The children are encouraged to re-create the text or to invent their own version. This book has been used in shared reading and class activities throughout the week.

On the noticeboard above the book corner is a display featuring Mo Willems. There is a picture of him with some brief facts about his life. There are also pictures of the covers of several of his books with a label which asks, 'How many books by Mo Willems have you read?' All the books are available in the book corner.

Also in the book corner is a large plastic box in which the children are encouraged to put the books they have read and really enjoyed. If children do not know what to read, they are encouraged to look in that box first. Often the teacher will put books in there too.

In the book corner is also a listening centre with earphones so children can choose a book and listen to the audio version.

The children are encouraged to re-enact the stories in the role-play area and in the small-play area. The role-play area is set up as a bus station for this week and in the small-play area are different types of vehicles and different animals. The children will often be heard saying things like, 'Don't let the cow drive the tractor'. This all relates to the overall theme for the half-term, which is Transport.

There are other examples of different kinds of texts around the classroom. All the displays are constantly used and referred to in lessons; children use them as a source of information. On the whiteboard the teacher has written the date and there are also several scribbled reminders which the teacher has written to herself to not forget to send messages home. The children know what these say and draw her attention to them at the end of the day. By the side of the whiteboard is a list of the activities of the day, in order. These are on laminated cards and at the beginning of each day the day's timetable is created with the children.

There are also opportunities for the children to create texts. There is one table for writing; it contains lots of paper of different colour, size and type, lots of different things to write with and a wire tray in which to put the finished writing. This is available for the children whenever they are free.

There is a music table which contains a few musical instruments and song books. On a stand is a copy of the song which the children have been learning that week. Children can be observed standing at this table playing the instruments and singing the song as they 'read' the musical notation.

There is also an alphabet display. Behind it is an alphabet chart with the lower case letters arranged in a rainbow shape.

Comment

This arrangement makes it easier for children, especially those with dyslexia, to find particular letters.

For other ideas look at:

Morris, M. and Smith, S. (2010) *Thirty-Three Ways to Help with Spelling: Supporting Children Who Struggle with Basic Skills*. London: Routledge.

There are also boxes of magnetic letters, arranged in sets of the letters the children have learned in phonics lessons. Some of these are joined where a grapheme consists of two or more letters. There are A4-sized magnetic boards in a box. Available for play are also wooden letters, sandpaper letters and letter-shape moulds. There are charts showing phoneme–grapheme correspondences and children are free to use these at any time.

Comment

As you read this observation and look around any classroom in which you find yourself, what are the messages that environment is giving out? The classroom I have described above tells me:

- Books are important – there is a space for books which is furnished with care and maintained.
- Readers make choices – the box of favourite books shows that different people will like different things.
- Authors write books – the emphasis on the author teaches children that books are essentially about communication.
- Composition is important – the opportunities to re-create stories through play are teaching children compositional skills.
- I can try out different things – the writing area allows children to experiment with writing.
- Different texts are for different purposes – enjoyment, reminding, informing, asking, and so on.

OBSERVATION: Year 5 classroom (ages 9 and 10)

The classroom is one of several which go off a long corridor in a building typical of those built in the 1960s. The wall opposite the door is almost all window and the tables are arranged in groups. At the back of the room is a sink.

There is no reading area as such, but there is a clearly defined class library. This consists of two bookcases arranged in an L-shape. One contains non-fiction books. These are coded according to a very simple Dewey system and there is a chart above the bookcase explaining this. The other bookcase contains fiction. This is mainly paperback novels of various sizes and thicknesses. I did not see any poetry books. There was a variety of authors represented on the shelves and a variety of genres that would appeal to different preferences. On a table next to this bookcase was a computer which was permanently on and had a selection of book covers and titles stuck around the screen. On the screen was a form:

```
Title:
Author:
Why you should read this book:
```

If the children had particularly enjoyed a book, they were invited to go and fill in this form and log it on the database of books that had been read by the class. The comments were unedited and brief; they often were in note form and contained lots of exclamation marks and question marks. If a child did not know what to read next, they could go through the database and select a book that one of their peers had already enjoyed. They were encouraged to go and ask the other child to elaborate on what was written.

Comment

The teacher told me that he had set this up for two reasons. First, he wanted to move away from the children having to write a book review every time they had read a book. Secondly, he wanted to create an environment where children were talking about books they had read and sharing opinions. In both respects this had worked. When I observed, he was considering making another database available of books which children had not enjoyed and had abandoned. What do you think about this? What would be the purpose of it?

This opportunity to respond to texts on screen was just one of the many types of texts evident in the classroom and a large number of them were on screen. The interactive whiteboard (IWB) was in constant use and it was an integral part of classroom activity, not just a resource for the teacher to use. The teacher used a tablet to write on as he walked around the classroom and this was recorded on the IWB; children were encouraged to record on the IWB or on one of the four computers in the room and were often flicking back and forwards between screens, some of which were created by them and some of which were from the Internet. Some of the displays consisted of these screens which had been printed out.

The whiteboard was used as a working wall and had notes and diagrams all over it. Teacher, teaching assistant and children wrote on it and, again, it was constantly referred to during lessons.

Comment

What were the children in this class learning about texts through the uses of written language in their classroom? It is a tradition in English primary classrooms that a display is always designed to look good – work is triple mounted, boards are backed with carefully chosen borders, and the font and size of print is carefully chosen. It is understandable why this is so; teachers want children to feel that their work is valued, they want to set good examples of standards of presentation and they want children to take pride in their work. I have observed the complete opposite in many primary classrooms in France. There I have seen notes made on flipcharts, the paper torn off and pinned on the wall with one drawing pin to be taken down the following day, referred to and added to. That was much as the whiteboard was used in the observed classroom. Consider these two almost extremes of examples of the printed word and identify the advantages and disadvantages of each. Is there a middle way?

Anybody visiting primary classrooms will soon realise that although there are some differences, there are many more similarities. Most primary classrooms contain the same things to a greater or lesser extent, for teaching and learning literacy. Brian Cambourne (2000:513) makes a very important point, however, when he says: 'artefacts are only valuable when students are engaged in meaningful tasks with the artefacts.' It could be said that the same argument applies to all texts used in a classroom, and so we need to be sure we understand what is meant by a 'meaningful task' in this context. How do you think Cambourne's argument relates to the views of Meek and Smith discussed earlier?

Summary

This chapter has encouraged you to think what we mean by the use of texts in the classroom. This is important because, although it is essential to teach children the skills of word recognition and language comprehension, it is imperative that teachers understand the impact that the texts which are used have on those processes.

- In reflecting on your own experiences of and creation of texts, you will have realised that texts come in many different forms. The essential characteristic of all texts is that their basic purpose is the communication of meaning. The nature of the text determines how that meaning will be created and/or accessed. Literacy teaching needs to take this into account.

- Planning for literacy teaching is best if texts are at its heart. Children will learn what makes for effective writing if they have talked about many examples of writing that have had an impact on them. Foregrounding the role of authors and writers shows children that effective writing involved many decisions which are often much more complex than the simple addition of more connectives or 'wow' words.
- Learning literacy involves knowing the purposes of different texts, and this is demonstrated by the way texts are used and displayed within the classroom. Giving children opportunities to create and read texts for authentic purposes will establish literacy as a powerful and essential tool.
- Reading aloud to children and talking with them about texts will introduce them to a range of authors and texts and will empower them to make their own choices as readers and writers.
- In order to do all this, teachers need to have a secure knowledge of texts which is relevant and up to date. This is challenging for teachers.
- There are experts in this who will help teachers, and the Schools Library Association will provide support and resources to teachers and schools.

The text is at the heart of literacy teaching and learning and must be considered in all our observations.

Further reading

Goodwin, P. (ed.) (2008) *Understanding Children's Books: A Guide for Education Professionals*. London: Sage.

Lockwood, M. (2008) *Promoting Reading for Pleasure in the Primary School*. London: Sage.

CHAPTER 2

TALK

Talk is an essential element of the learning process but it is sometimes difficult to observe and to see what lies beneath the words. The observations in this chapter demonstrate talk in different contexts and how adults can help or hinder.

If you were asked to identify what is the most important thing that helps you to learn, I wonder what you would say. When we teach, it is very easy to focus on things like preparing exactly the right worksheets, thinking how we are going to explain a topic, having lots of management and organisational strategies up our sleeves and carefully differentiating all the activities. All these things are vitally important and key in becoming an effective teacher, but the most important way in which we all learn is through talk. Why do I say this? Alexander (2004: 9) says 'Children … need to talk and experience a rich diet of spoken language, in order to think and to learn'. This is difficult to achieve and many teachers struggle to provide this rich diet of spoken language in their classrooms. Why is it important and what happens when children talk?

Research over the past few decades has convinced us of the incontrovertible link between talk and thought. Children's cognitive development is encouraged or hampered by the types of language they have encountered and the contexts in which they have encountered it. Halliday (1993) argued that learning language was about learning how to learn.

Recent research in neuroscience confirms that talk serves a powerful function in helping the brain to build connections and thus expand its capability. The primary stage of education seems to be the time in which the brain is actively developing its capacity for learning and has a strong ability to learn language. The relevance of this research for teachers is to emphasise the importance of teaching. Teachers are no longer just facilitators, providing stimulating environments, resources and activities, pressing the 'go' button and waiting for it to happen. The interactions teachers have with children are of vital importance. In other words, what you say to children and how you say it is vitally important, as are, if not more so, the opportunities you give children to talk themselves.

Read
Goswami, U. (2006) 'The brain in the classroom? The state of the art', *Developmental Science*, 8, 467–9.

One of the strongest influences on primary education in the past was the work of Piaget, a psychologist interested in the development of thinking, reasoning and understanding. His view of children as meaning-makers interacting with the environment in which they find themselves, was the prompt for much of child-centred education. Children were placed in a stimulating environment and the teacher acted as facilitator, helping the children to make connections between what they already knew and new experiences.

The thinking of the Russian psychologist, Vygotsky, challenged this idea of the child working alone to develop understanding and argues that social interaction is at the heart of development. Language is the key tool which allows the child to understand experiences and a child's interactions with those who are more experienced help the child to make sense of the world.

The term 'scaffolding' was first used by Bruner to describe those interactions between adult and child. Adults should provide the link between what the child can do and understand independently and what she or he can do with the support of a more experienced other. In other words, the teacher should use language in a way that challenges the child's thinking and extends understanding.

If you were to teach me how to tie my shoelaces it would be a waste of time. You might plan a superb lesson which was interactive, used resources creatively, engaged me completely and was managed smoothly, but it would all be to no avail because I am already able to tie my shoelaces and can do so independently. You might plan a similarly effective and exciting lesson to teach me the principles of nuclear physics and it would also be a waste of time – not because I already know about nuclear physics but because I have no understanding of physics at all and nuclear physics is way too advanced for me and my level of understanding. Teaching is about finding the level which is the next step forward from what is already known by the pupil. Vygotsky named this the 'zone of proximal development'.

Bruner and Vygotsky would say that providing the right context with stimulating resources would not be enough but that an effective teacher would need to be with me in my zone of proximal development talking me through, explaining and guiding. It is the talk that is vital. This interaction has been described as 'scaffolding'; it is the verbal support which allows a child to carry out a task which they would not be able to do alone. Wood et al. (1976) described six features of effective scaffolding:

- 'recruitment' or stimulating interest in the task
- 'reduction in degrees of freedom' or simplifying the task, perhaps by breaking it down into stages
- 'direction maintenance' or focusing children by reminding them of the goal
- 'marking critical features' or pointing out key things to do and/or showing the child other ways of doing parts of the task
- 'frustration control' or managing the child's frustration during the task
- 'demonstration' or showing a way of doing the task.

Consider these characteristics as you look at the observations in this chapter.

> **Read**
>
> Maybin, J., Mercer, N. and Stierer, B. (1992) 'Scaffolding learning in the classroom', in K. Norman (ed.), *Thinking Voices: The Work of the National Oracy Project.* London: Hodder. pp. 186–95.

OBSERVATION: Year 1 children in free play (ages 5 and 6)

The following observation is of 5- and 6-year-old children in a free-play activity. They are working independently and talking with each other. On two occasions different adults intervene and ask questions. Use this observation to reflect on the role of the adult in relation to what you have read about the nature of scaffolding.

In this school three parallel Year 1 classes spend 45 minutes most afternoons in free-play activities. They use a large outdoor area, the three small classrooms and a large shared area. This is known as 'Sunshine Time'. There are adults around but on the afternoon I observed they were not normally joining in the children's play but were spending their time reading with individual children.

I watched five children – four girls and a boy – working together. They were sticking coloured sheets of A4 paper together with sticky tape into a long strip. They were individually working on each piece of paper but had clearly planned it together. I started to listen when this activity had been going on for some time.

Child 1:   We don't have time to stick things on. Let's just draw.
Child 2:   Come on, we've got work to do. The more drawing, the more beautiful.

(pause while the children are busily each drawing on their individual sheets of paper)

> ### Comment
> Notice how the children are working alongside each other in what is often known as parallel play. They have planned a project together and now are individually working on their separate parts of the whole. When alone, the children do not talk much. As the adult approaches, they invite her to look at their work. What do you think of the adult's comments? What might you have said in the same circumstances?

An adult walks past.

Child 3:   Miss S., look at this. This is the longest longest city.
Miss S: Is it taller than our metre man? Is it taller than me? (Miss S lies down on the floor alongside the strips of paper. A child lies down on the other side.) Is it taller than Charlie?
Child 3:   It's taller than everything.

> ### Comment
> Notice how the adult changes the nature and focus of the talk. Previously the children were excited about their project and were discussing the process of completing it. The adult immediately turned it into a teaching situation, comparing the length of the paper with people. She did not comment on what the project was in the children's imagination but only on what she perceived she could use it for. How do you think the children would react to this focus of questioning? Child 3 was the only child who responded here. Consider this in relation to Child's 3 talk in the following extract.

The adult then left and the children carried on talking together.

Child 2: Seven more to go.
Child 1: I'll do the pink one.
Child 2: There are seven more to go. (Picks it up) Look at that – all of that.
Child 3: Who is helping?
Child 5: Where is the Sellotape?
Child 1: Um – where is it? There.
Child 3: My arm is killing me. I'm doing so much drawing without a rest.
Child 2: No more paper on this.
Child 5: I'm going to get my own paper – not yours.

Comment

The children seem to have ignored the adult's intervention and carried on as before! Look at the different roles the children are taking and consider how what they are saying reflects these roles. For example, Child 3 is using language to draw attention to what she is doing. Her question about who is helping serves to draw attention to the fact that not many children are and her later comment emphasises her own role on the project. She is using language to assert her own role in the project. How would you describe the roles of Children 2 and 5?

Another adult then approached.

Teacher: Is it a huge poster? A banner?
Child 3: It's a rainbow city.
Teacher: Is each sheet a part of the city? And what's in the city? Is it an imaginary city?
(Pause. The children do not respond to the questions but carry on working.)
Teacher: That's really long.
Child 3: Yea. Everybody helped and it's really long.

Comment

Look at the questions the teacher was asking and think how they were supporting and challenging the children's thinking. Why did the teacher ask the first question instead of asking the children directly what it was they were making? Often teachers do not like to admit that they do not recognise what children are making, and make assumptions. When she was told what the project was, the teacher then asked three questions in rapid succession without pausing for the children to answer. The children ignored her, except

(Continues)

(Continued)

for Child 3, who again was the only child who responded to the teacher. Think how you could engage in conversation with the children to encourage them to talk more purposefully.

If you consider the above observation there are some key points we can learn about what happens when young children are engaged in free-play activities.

- Children's imagination and creativity is strong and vibrant. These children were creating their own world and using the resources available for their own purposes. In his foreword to Pahl and Rowsell (2005), Allan Luke talks about the 'epistemological diversity' to be found in classrooms. What does this mean to you? It can be argued, and Luke does this, that the curriculum and pedagogy in many classrooms is a sort of 'educational fundamentalism' which reduces learning in general and literacy learning in particular to a much simpler and slower approach to simpler and basic texts and modes of communication. In contrast, according to Luke, 'students bring to classrooms complex, multiple and blended background knowledges, identities and discourses, constructing identity and practice from a range of scripts' (in Pahl and Roswell, 2005: xiii). What does this mean in relation to the observation? It means that we need to allow the children to tell us what they are creating and how they are creating it. Both adults resorted to discussion of measurement of length because the children were creating something long. That was not what was foremost in the children's thinking. They were using other knowledges and experiences to create their world. What are the implications for teachers in how they respond and talk with children?
- Children think and operate in narrative. Story is the focus of the final chapter and we will return to consider its importance there but, for now, consider how these children were creating their own story. Rosen (1984) describes story as a cognitive tool which helps us to understand our world. Is this what was going on here? Look again at the roles the different children took. Are they creating a shared world? Whose world is it?
- Adult interventions can open up but also close down conversations and opportunities to challenge and extend children's learning. We will return to this point later in the chapter but for now, reflect on the adults' questioning in the observation above and think how the questions might be modified to impact on children's learning. Consider also how a change in the way the adult talks might influence the role the adult plays in the learning episode. Try and reword the conversation according to the characteristics of scaffolding.

OBSERVATION: Year 6 children talking (ages 10 and 11)

The next observation is of children in Year 6 (ages 10 and 11). They also were talking with each other without much intervention from the teacher in a structured Philosophy for Children session. The rationale behind Philosophy for Children is an approach called 'community of enquiry'. It is designed to encourage children to think, reason and to make sense of arguments and counter arguments. Its principles are:

- critical thinking – children who are able to make distinctions, connections, comparisons and give reasons
- creative thinking – constructing alternative scenarios and explanations and making necessary links between reasons and conclusions
- caring – feeling safe to take risks and strengthening personal values
- collaborating – discussion making thinking a social activity.

It can be seen that this approach is Vygotskian in its underpinning and so we are justified in looking for evidence of challenge and scaffolding by the more experienced in the interaction. In this session the children were sitting on the floor in a circle – all the furniture had been pushed to one side to make space. This was the second lesson of a series. In the first lesson the teacher had read the children a story and they had identified a question which arose from it for them. This was 'Should you risk everything for your dreams?'

Each child had three opportunities to speak, signified by holding up three fingers. The child who spoke chose the next child to speak. The teacher began by reminding them of her role; she used the word 'facilitator' and said that if they lost their way she would bring them back on track. She then chose one person from the group whose question had been chosen to start.

The discussion lasted half an hour and I will give just some examples, starting with the beginning. Each paragraph is a new speaker; each speaker nominated the next speaker by name and I have left that out of the transcript.

I think it depends what your dreams are and it depends what you're risking. If it's your life, it's probably, you really shouldn't. If you can get it without really trying it really isn't a risk but if it is a really big thing that you've always really wanted it's worth the risk.

I think you shouldn't because if you're risking something like 50p there's a high chance you probably would. But if it's something where the risk is reasonably high although it could not affect you it could affect other people so in that way I think you shouldn't.

I think you shouldn't because if you say you're a thief you can get in real trouble.

I reckon you shouldn't but maybe it depends on what it is and what it's worth. If it's your life that's a different thing but if say you're risking 1p then that would, then you might want to do it if you've got a chance like of winning the lottery.

It depends on how risky it is. If someone says if you steal something from me – it depends on what they say they're going to do.

You shouldn't risk something if it affects other people because that might be causing people harm. If it only affects you, like maybe you dying, then that's the step you're taking.

I would think twice. If you do succeed then what are you going to get for it. It depends how high you're willing to go really. It depends on what you're going to get if you go to the next level.

I disagree with S. Because if it's something you really want, you shouldn't risk, for example, somebody's life or because that might be overdoing it.

Comment

This is the first time a child has made an explicit reference back to somebody else's comment. The reference back was not to the previous statement but to the first one made. The child had to wait until she was chosen to make her point. What are the implications of this for the construction of a dialogue?

I think that if it's a bad thing, like if you want to win a prize by cheating, then I don't think you should. But if you want to do something like saving red squirrels for example, then maybe you should because although you won't win anything you'll be saving something else.

Well I agree with J because he said if it affects other people I wouldn't do it but if you think about what you want to win and you want to risk your life saving your country that's good.

I agree with M because when you think about it, when you actually have a dream would you be helping somebody else? You could end up being greedy because if you're doing it just for yourself for say fame or money or things like that then it's really selfish and not very nice then if you do something to help people which could change the world, you could risk some things to help people.

Well I think that it depends on if you do succeed and it maybe makes you famous or something I would try and get benefit for other people as well, so like maybe help a charity or stuff. If you just want to be famous and not do anything about it but just earn money then I wouldn't do it.

If you had a dream and you got it by stealing you might get a worser dream like gaol.

The discussion so far had taken 10 minutes and the teacher then intervened. She said:

> Right, I'm just going to butt in here for a minute. Supposing you wanted something very very special in your life – a car or a football kit or jewellery – and you knew somebody who had loads of money – would you think that it would be OK – somehow – to steal from that person who had so much money to get what you would want – what you would dream of? Is it OK to do it? Or if you had somebody who didn't have any money at all, would you still do the same thing from them? Would you steal from them or … so think about that sort of thing. The rights and wrongs.

The children's discussion continued:

> I think it's wrong to steal from someone who's like rich because you never know what they're going to do with the money. Say if they give it to charity they can help more than one person.

> Well I disagree with somebody about wars, because what does it help, what does it do if you kill loads of people to make the world better, it's a smaller place really and maybe it's just making people a bit lonely if they've lost their families.

> I didn't say you'd have war. If you're in a war and your country is really poor and you're invaded like loads of times and you really want to win this war so you won't have any more problems.

Barnes and Todd (1977) used the term 'exploratory talk' to describe talk where things are achieved. Mercer (1995) developed this idea and identified characteristics of this type of talk:

- Ideas are engaged with critically but encouragingly.
- Statements are considered and challenged but there is always explicit justification and alternative proposals.
- Ideas and viewpoints are made public and the talk provides evidence of reasoning.
- The discussion moves towards joint agreement.

The discussion in the observation goes some way towards addressing these issues but there are times, maybe, when the imposed structure gets in the way of the development of thinking.

Task

Look at the following resource for other ideas for using talk to develop thinking skills.

Dawes, L., Mercer, N. and Wegerif, R. (2000) *Thinking Together: Activities for Teachers and Children at Key Stage 2*. Birmingham: Questions Publishing.

Dialogic teaching

At this point it is helpful to consider the notion of 'dialogic teaching' and begin to focus on the role of the teacher in helping children to use talk effectively. Traditionally, teachers have not been good at opening up opportunities for children to talk. You will have observed many lessons, I am sure, where it seemed as though the teacher was doing most of the talking. Research backs up this impression (Bennett and Desforges 1984; Galton and Simon 1980; Mroz et al., 2000). Talk in classrooms has often been used to see if children 'know' the correct answer and rather than creating opportunities for exploration, teacher questions are testing. In real life we usually ask questions for a variety of reasons: to find some information, to see what somebody else thinks, to question an idea or viewpoint, to request something, and so on. In classrooms teachers often ask questions to see if children remember what they have been taught and these questions can often lead to a bizarre 'guess what's in my mind' game. We can define questions by the extent to which they are open or closed. Closed questions have only one expected answer; open questions create opportunities for dialogue and thought. It is easy to identify which types of questions are generally the most effective in the classroom.

Sinclair and Coulthard (1975) described a common classroom interaction between teacher and child as IRF (Initiate, Respond, Follow-up); the teacher initiates by asking a question, the child responds and the teacher gives a brief follow-up. Little cognitive challenge takes place and the questions tend to be closed and used to check knowledge gained. Since the introduction of the literacy and numeracy frameworks, in 1998 and 1999 respectively, there has been much emphasis placed on what is described as 'whole-class interactive teaching'. Teachers have been encouraged to plan lessons which are pacey, discursive and challenging. There are many teaching strategies put forward to encourage this type of teaching and to ensure that all children contribute in whole-class discussion:

- Seating arrangements – how do you think the physical layout of a classroom supports or hinders talk?
- Using props – individual whiteboards, puppets, an object to hold, counters or the hand signals used in the previous observation.
- Involving everybody – no hands up but the speaker is selected by the teacher, using a prop to choose the next speaker – named lolly sticks, talking hat, number grid.
- Alternatives to teacher–child interactions – talking partners, time to talk.
- Structures – thinking time, group spokesperson reporting back.

Task
Look for examples of these strategies when you observe lessons, and reflect on how they encourage exploratory talk in those lessons.

Unfortunately it seems that these strategies have had little impact on classroom practice. Smith et al. found that, 'teachers spent the majority of their time either explaining or using highly structured question and answer sequences … most of the questions were of a low cognitive level designed to funnel pupils' response towards a required answer' (2004: 408).

Read
Smith, F., Hardman, F., Wall, K. and Mroz, M. (2004) 'Interactive whole class teaching in the National Literacy and Numeracy Strategies', *British Educational Research Journal*, 30(3): 403–19.

Robin Alexander proposes that it is, therefore, the cognitive challenge of classroom talk which needs to be addressed rather than organisation and pace of whole-class teaching. He introduces the term 'dialogic teaching' as a way forward. His idea is grounded in the works of Bruner (1996), who argued that it is discussion and collaboration which lead to understanding, and of Wells (1999), who described learning classrooms as 'community of enquiry'. The notion also links closely with Mercer's idea of 'interthinking' discussed earlier. Alexander identifies five key principles of dialogic teaching:

- Collective: teacher and children addressing learning tasks together
- Reciprocal: teachers and children listening to each other
- Supportive: children free to articulate their own ideas without fear, helping each other to understand
- Cumulative: teachers and children building on each others' ideas to create coherent thinking
- Purposeful: teaching has particular educational goals in mind. (Alexander 2008: 28)

OBSERVATION: Art lesson with Year 3 class (ages 7 and 8)

The staff of this urban school were focusing on talk during the term in which this observation was made. They were looking at ways of creating opportunities for cognitively challenging talk. This lesson was part of a series in which the children had been looking at the work of graphic designers and digital artists. The overarching theme of the term's work across the curriculum was 'Extreme Environments'. The aim of the observed lesson was to design a jungle animal structure using digitally designed materials. The teacher's intention for herself was to use questions which would challenge and generate thinking. The whole-class part of the lesson involved looking at pictorial examples of sculptures made from digitally created materials, for example, a table made from bottles and a parrot made from bus tickets.

Extensive use was made of 'talking partners'. The children were put into pairs by the teacher and every time there was whole-class work each child sat next to their talking partner. They worked with the same talking partner for two weeks and then the teacher changed the pairings.

Comment

The way in which talk partners are selected can make a big difference to the quality of the talk. Think about a class you know well and identify as many different ways as possible of allocating talk partners. Now think of the positive and less positive consequences of these decisions. Do you think keeping the same partners over time is better than allocating specific partners for particular tasks?

Lancashire County Council wrote a useful pamphlet, 'Talk Partners' which you can access through Google.

The teacher asked lots of questions in the whole class discussion and the children were engaged and clearly thinking hard. The first question came after they had looked at pictures of several very different images of graphic art.

What do all of these images have in common?

Answers varied but the class, after about 5 minutes' discussion, worked out that all the images had been graphically designed.

Comment

What enabled the children to be able to come to this conclusion together? It could be argued that the question is closed – it is asking the children to find the answer. However, it is a challenge and the children rose to it. On the surface the images were very different. The question required them to reflect critically on what they had seen and to draw on their previous experiences. During the discussion the teacher took a back seat, only joining in to ask for justification or clarification, and on one occasion to question a response. The children engaged with each other. We could apply all five principles of dialogic teaching to this. This happened not only because of the type of question which was asked but the role the teacher adopted during the conversation. Unlike the teacher in the Philosophy for Children discussion she did not take a back seat but was involved in extending and challenging thinking. She was more than a facilitator but did not direct. This was a true discussion as defined by Alexander, where there was 'the exchange of ideas with a view to sharing information and solving problems' (2008: 30).

The PowerPoint slide then looked at different examples of sculptures made from graphically generated materials. The first slide was a picture of a sculpture of a polar bear, at the Eden Project in Cornwall, made from plastic carrier bags. There was some discussion about what the bear was made from and the teacher continually referred the children back to the picture to look for evidence to support their viewpoints. Note how she used a visual image as a 'text' in much the same way as a written text would be used.

She then asked the children the question, 'Why did they use carrier bags and not cardboard boxes to make the polar bear?' The children discussed this in their talking partners and after about five minutes the teacher asked, 'What does your talking partner think?' The children then reported back using the ideas of their partner.

Comment

Why do you think the teacher did this? If a child is shy about sharing their own ideas with the whole class, it is much easier to report on somebody else's views. It also ensured that the children listened carefully to their partners and gave them practise in identifying the key points.

Alexander identifies some characteristics of dialogic teaching and it is useful to use this as a framework for analysing interactions we observe in classrooms. You can see them fully and read more about dialogic teaching in the following text:

Alexander, R. (2008) *Towards Dialogic Teaching: Rethinking Classroom Talk.* 4th edn. Thirsk: Dialogos.

The next image was a parrot constructed out of bus tickets. Read straight through the dialogue first; it might help to read it aloud. It went like this:

Child 1:   I think it's made of sticks.

Child 2:   No, it's too shiny for sticks. I think it's made of plastic.

Child 3:   The feathers look like they're made out of bus tickets.

Teacher: What makes you think they're made from bus tickets?

Child 3:   The yellow things that you have on bus tickets. They're long and bus tickets are long.

Child 4:   If you look closely you can see a bit of black.

Child 5:   Is it the writing on the tickets?

Child 3:   I think it must be.

Teacher: What do you notice about the ways they've used the bus tickets?

Child 2:   They've done lots of different layers.

Child 4:   That makes it look more like feathers.

Now let us look more closely at the sort of talk used and how the comments of each contributor fitted together to construct a cohesive argument. My analysis is based on Alexander's characteristics of dialogic teaching. You may not agree with me; if not, look carefully at the 'text' to justify your own viewpoint.

Child 1:   I think it's made of sticks.

Comment

This child is using talk to speculate. The comment acts as a springboard for other comments.

Child 2:   No, it's too shiny for sticks. I think it's made of plastic.

Comment

This child has clearly listened to the previous comment and is responding to it. The fact that she or he is expressing disagreement indicates confidence to express a viewpoint without the need to always be correct. The disagreement is justified; the child gives a reason for the differing viewpoint.

Child 3:   The feathers look like they're made out of bus tickets.

Comment

A clear and coherent line of argument is developing with the children collaborating to try and solve the problem of deciding what the sculpture is made from. Child 3 slightly changes the style of comment but again is speculating.

Teacher: What makes you think they're made from bus tickets?

Comment

The question asked by the teacher is firmly part of the ongoing dialogue, building on previous comments and taking them further. The question 'elicits evidence of children's understanding' and 'prompts and challenges thinking and reasoning'. The question is framed in such a way that the answer cannot be wrong; the child is asked to give reasons for an opinion which is accepted as a valid opinion.

Child 3:   The yellow things that you have on bus tickets. They're long and bus tickets are long.

Comment

The child's response is less clear without contextual clues to help understanding, but it is a definite response to the teacher's question and provides the information required to justify the expressed opinion. This child is drawing on his own experience of bus tickets to provide evidence and justification.

Child 4:   If you look closely you can see a bit of black.

Comment

Child 4 develops the argument further and supplies additional evidence. There is no competition in this dialogic problem-solving; the children are collaborating to find an answer. Child 4 is building on previous contributions and in turn the following statement shows another child doing the same.

Child 5:   Is it the writing on the tickets?
Child 3:   I think it must be.

Comment

Another child enters the discussion and asks a question. It is a feature of dialogic teaching that it is not just teachers who ask questions. Asking an appropriate question can be a cognitively challenging task and Child 5 shows that she or he has been following the discussion, is building on previous evidence and is fully engaged in the task. Alexander argues that in dialogic teaching, 'those who are not speaking at a given time participate no less actively by listening, looking, reflecting and evaluating' (2008: 42). This is the first contribution made by Child 5 but she or he has been an active participant in the debate. Child 3 responds; the question was addressed to the group as a whole not necessarily to the teacher.

Teacher: What do you notice about the ways they've used the bus tickets?

Comment

Now that the materials used have been established by the group the teacher moves the focus on by establishing a slightly different line of enquiry. Again, she focuses the children's attention on the picture and asks what they can see. This question serves a slightly different purpose from the teacher's previous one; she is bringing them back to the 'text' and challenging them to take the idea of using bus tickets even further. The responses below show that the children pick up on this and begin to discuss method of construction rather than materials.

Child 2:   They've done lots of different layers.
Child 4:   That makes it look more like feathers.

Comment

The first response is a direct answer to the teacher's question and the following comment by Child 4 expands on this and speculates on the outcome of the layering. This is another example of the interaction building on previous comments and collaboration in solving the problem.

One of the most significant characteristics of the interaction above was the balance of talk by the teacher and talk by the children. The children talked more than the teacher. It was also clear when observing that, although the dialogue moved forwards, there were also times of silence when the children were looking carefully at the picture and reflecting. The teacher did not feel tempted to fill that silence but allowed for thinking time.

Let us match this dialogue against the principles of dialogic teaching described above.

- Collectivity – the children were working together to work out what the sculpture was made from and how it was made.
- Reciprocal – the children were listening to each other and responding and building on each other's comments. The teacher was also listening and played an almost equal role in the dialogue.
- Supportive – the children appeared to be confident in expressing their own ideas, in asking questions and in supporting each other.
- Cumulative – the children built on each other's comments, extending ideas and moving thinking forward. The teacher's contributions also did this without dominating or denigrating anything anybody else had said.
- Purposeful – this was planned with a clear purpose in mind. The teacher reviewed the comments and her own comments moved them forward according to her purpose, as evidenced in her second question.

Reflection

Do you think this is an example of dialogic teaching. If so, then what is your evidence for that claim? If not, what would you want to see to justify the description?

OBSERVATION: Conversation between a teacher and a Reception child about a self-chosen book (age 5)

Let us now move on to look at interactions between a teacher and a 5-year-old little boy called Theo. The first conversation happened when the child chose a book to read and discuss with his teacher. He chose *Owl Babies* by Martin Waddell and it might help if you have the book with you as you read this dialogue.

Teacher: Why did you choose this book Theo?

Theo: Well my mummy always reads this to me that's why I know it. (looking at the front cover) These are baby owls. (opens the book) This is their feathers, can you see the pattern?

> **Comment**
> Theo has chosen a well-loved book and one which he knows really well. This enables him to take control of the conversation and to initiate topics of discussion and ask questions. He is in the role of expert. What impact do you think this has on Theo's talk?

Teacher: Oh, yes, I can!

Theo: (turns to first page and compares background to previous page) See it's the same but it's their mummy's feathers. This is Sarah, this is Percy and that one's Bill. ('reading' the words) They lived in a tree with their mummy. (turns page) Oh no they woke up 'cause they couldn't sleep, they were hungry, their mummy had gone so they're so sad. Look at Percy's face.

> **Comment**
> Theo is half 'reading' the book by remembering the text from when his mother has read it to him and half commenting on it. This dialogue could have been in the following chapter on reading. Why do you think I chose to put it in the chapter on talk?

Teacher: Mmm. He does look a bit sad. How do you think Sarah and Bill are feeling?

> **Comment**
> Look carefully at what the teacher says. She responds to Theo's instruction to look at Percy's face and then asks Theo to look at Sarah and Bill. How do you think the teacher could have responded in a way which would extend the child's thinking more? Look at how Theo responds to the question below. See how he is drawing on his past experiences to make his answer. How could the teacher focus his thinking to draw on evidence from the text?

Theo: Well, I think they might be a bit sad too, but they might not because they're bigger than Bill. (turns page) They're thinking about their mummy. Percy think she might get a fox. ('reads' the words) I want my mummy. (turns the page and 'reads' the words) But mummy owl didn't come. (turns the page and 'reads') A big branch for Sarah a small branch for Percy and a bit of ivy for Bill. I want my mummy. (turns page) They snuggled together 'cause they were a little bit afraid. That's Bill in the middle 'cause he's the smallest. (turns page and 'reads') So they closed their eyes and wishes for their mummy to come. And she did. (turns two pages studying the pictures) Owls come out at night and I saw a hedgehog in my garden and it was in this pile of leaves and it stayed there all the time, I think it was a whole day. And it was sort of this big (uses hands) with lots of spiky prickles.

Comment
Here Theo is relating a real life experience to the text. The idea of owls being nocturnal has reminded him of the hedgehogs he saw in his garden. How does the teacher respond to this? What do you think about her response?

Teacher: Did it look like the one we saw this morning?

Comment
The teacher follows Theo's thoughts about the hedgehog but Theo does not seem to want to take it any further and returns to the book. Note how the teacher does not push her question but allows Theo to carry on reading the book.

Theo: Well sort of. (returns to book) Mummy! Look Bill almost jumped up and fell off and Bill he's jumping up too 'cause he's pleased to see his Mummy! My mummy always reads this book to me that's why I know it so well. (turns page and reads) What's all the fuss! You knew I'd come back. I love my mummy!

Teacher: Why do you like this book Theo?

Theo: Well I know this book 'cause my mummy picks it for me and reads it to me and that's why I know it.

> **Comment**
> The teacher almost repeats her first question but this time asking why Theo likes the book. Theo does not really answer the question and the teacher lets it go. If you were this teacher, what question would you ask to help Theo really think about why he likes the book. The teacher here has let go an opportunity to challenge Theo's thinking.

This delightful conversation is about a book which Theo clearly knows very well and the way he makes sense of it is closely bound up with his own emotional experiences of his mummy reading to him. Reading this book is a very personal act and so it can be more difficult to articulate those feelings.

Let us focus on the teacher's comments and questions. At the start Theo is very much in control and the teacher responds as an equal, sharing in the enjoyment. From then on, however, her questions become very teacherly. She invites him to speculate, reminds him of relevant past experiences and repeats her question about why he chose the book. There are many ways in which these are not bad questions and it is more a case of good questions asked at the wrong time. If you try reading this conversation aloud, it might well feel as though the teacher's questions do not sit easily in the natural flow of Theo's talk. The teacher does not appear to be listening and responding to Theo and her questions do not always build on what he was saying. This observation reminds us of a key principle of talking with children – listen to them first!

OBSERVATION: Conversation 2 with child in Reception class (age 5)

Theo and his class had had a visit from a member of a bat sanctuary who showed a visual presentation on bats and then brought out two bats to show to the children. The presentation was long (15 minutes) for the age of children; the pictures were clear and informative but a lot of the language used was subject specific and not explained to the children. After the visit, an adult had the following conversation with Theo:

Adult: Hi Theo. I wonder if you could help me. I couldn't see or hear everything that was going on in the hall with the bats and I have to write some things down about it. Can you help me please?

Theo: Well what I found out was that bats chew off their wings or their tails sometimes when they're hungry. Well, I'm not quite sure but I think it's when they are hungry. And they live in attics and bees can live in attics. And there are bats that eat fruit and there are bats that eat insects and bats that eat moths and some nibble on birds.

Adult: What makes you think they eat their tails and wings?

Theo: Well, the man told me, but I think he got it wrong.

Adult: Maybe he meant that when the bats eat upside down, they eat off their tails and wings using them a bit like plates.

Theo: Mmmmm, yes I think that could be right.

Adult: Did you find out anything about the noises the bats make?

Theo: Well the lady had a machine and it had a recording of a bat and it says something and it comes back to them. And if the echo went on and on and on it wouldn't be an insect.

Adult: So what do bats do in winter?

Theo: Well they sleep in the winter cause there's no food – just like the poor people don't have any food or toys or anything, but at Christmas me and mummy, we get some of my toys and an old teddy and we put it in a shoe box and then we leave it out for Father Christmas and then whoosh it goes and into the truck and off to Gambia. We also put in some tissues so the poor people can have a good blow.

Adult: So can you tell me anything about baby bats?

Theo: The baby bats when they're borned they stay with their mummies and if their mummies leave them they are all upset.

Adult: So do the babies have fur or anything when they're born?

Theo: Yes they've got fur and they hang upside down next to their mummies.

Adult: So what do the babies eat?

Theo: Well some eat fruit, some eat moths and some eat insects.

Adult: Can you tell me about the bats that you saw?

Theo: Well he wanted to fly but the man had hold of him 'cause he had a poorly wing and the bat was a bit agitated. I got to stroke him and it was soft and he had tiny ears and the man was holding him by the wings so that's why it's agitated.

Comment

What is your initial response to that conversation? Do you think it was a conversation? Remember the research of Sinclair and Coulthard who described the initiation–response–feedback routine which is so common in classroom talk? Go back over this conversation and try and match the contributions to that pattern. I think you will find that as the conversation progresses there is initiation from the teacher, response from Theo but little if any feedback from the teacher. What is the purpose of this conversation? It seems to be to test Theo to see if he remembered what he had been told in the presentation. Was Theo cognitively challenged at all?

Reflect on this observation and use it to remind yourself of what you know about effective talk in the classroom.

Read

Eke, R. and Lee, J. (2009) *Using Talk Effectively in the Primary Classroom.* London: David Fulton.

Eke and Lee identify the particular characteristics of school talk as opposed to 'normal' talk; they argue that school talk is often very context bound. Other differences are:

- In normal talk speakers often skip from theme to theme whereas in school talk interactions are normally themed.
- In normal talk invitations to do something can be refused but this is not the case in school talk.
- In normal conversation speakers often overlap and interrupt each other but the rules for classroom talk tend not to allow this.
- Teacher talk often regulates and instructs; normal talk is between equals.

Teachers often claim that some children come to school familiar with the way in which language is used in school, while others operate only in the 'real world'. Eke and Lee use the term 'pedagogic communication' to describe 'the way teachers use talk to make the potential knowledge and skills actual in the classroom' (2009: 22). Language becomes the action in the classroom. Nystrand emphasises this point when he says, 'what ultimately counts is the extent to which instruction requires students to think, not just report someone else's thinking' (1997: 73). It is this which must be the aim of all effective teachers.

Summary

Why is talk so important? There are many reasons:

- It is our main means of communication.
- It is used to create relationships.
- It creates and maintains cultural identity.
- It plays a key role in the development of the brain.
- It is linked to the development of thinking.
- It promotes and helps learning and raises achievement.
- It makes active citizens who can make and justify choices.

How do we help and teach children to use language in this way? As teachers, much of children's use of language in the classroom is influenced by our language. We have seen that the most effective language by teachers, whether talking with individuals or whole classes, follows the principles of dialogic teaching:

- collective
- reciprocal
- supportive
- cumulative
- purposeful.

We can plan for this in all different organisational contexts but it also means that we must listen and respond to children. Alexander argues we must also listen to other professionals and together develop our understanding of professional practice: 'The critical question concerns the impact of talk on learning ... We must know where the talk is going, and do what is required to lead it there. That requires us to have a clear sense of purpose and a firm grasp of the content to be covered' (2008: 49).

Further reading

Goodwin, P. (ed.) (2001) *The Articulate Classroom: Talking and Learning in the Primary Classroom.* London: David Fulton.

CHAPTER 3

TEACHING READING

Teaching reading is a high priority and one that is politically sensitive. The observations in this chapter look at different aspects of teaching reading and consider how these fit together to support the development of 'readers'..

The first questions we need to ask ourselves when we begin to think about how to teach children to read are, 'What are we actually teaching? What is reading and how will we know when we have taught it?' These questions are not as straightforward as you might first imagine. Take a few moments to think about them and if possible to discuss possible answers with a friend.

What is reading?

It is helpful in answering this question to think back over all the reading experiences you have had over the last 24 hours. You will have read many different sorts of things and you will have read them for different reasons and in different ways. Sometimes you will have skimmed over a text quickly just to get the sense of what it is about but on other occasions you will have read each word very carefully and slowly.

> **Task**
> List everything you read in the last 24 hours and note how and why you read it.

I am sure you have had the experience of reading a text to yourself and getting to the end of the page to realise that you were actually thinking about something completely different. You were able to decode the words but did not engage with the meaning at all. It would be difficult to say that you had really 'read' that text. Similarly, you may have read something and skipped over some difficult or new words, thinking you had a broad idea of the meaning. However, in discussion with somebody else you realise that you had either got the wrong end of the stick or had missed some key part of the text because you could not read an important word. These two elements of reading, the word identification and the comprehension or understanding, are both essential and need to be taught together. Knowing how that is done is a complex issue and every day in classrooms teachers are making professional judgements about the needs of children and how to address them.

The teaching of reading is a highly political issue and different governments have commissioned reports and issued policy statements on how it is to be taught. It is important that teachers understand the reading process and are able to make their own professional judgements about the teaching approaches which suit the different children in their class. It does not take long to appreciate that one approach to teaching reading does not suit all and teachers need to be able to assess and make decisions which are informed by research and experience.

There is often a tension between policy-making and classroom practice and the extent to which pedagogy is determined by research evidence. This is complicated in the teaching of reading because the sources of evidence come from different research traditions and so place different emphases on the various aspects of the reading process. It is important that you understand these perspectives as they all have something to offer you in support of those professional decisions you make in the classroom.

- If you read anything by Ken or Yetta Goodman, Don Holdaway or Margaret Meek you will notice an emphasis on reading as a process of making meaning from the text. This psycholinguistic approach looked at how experienced readers behaved and argued that beginning readers need to be shown how to behave in the same way. Thus, it is said that reading development does not happen in a staged way. Goodman (1992) identified three sources of information in a text that readers draw on: graphophonic (the relationship between the phonemes and the graphemes – the sounds of language and their written representation), syntactic (the grammatical structure of the written language – the way the different elements fit together) and semantic – the meaning of the text within the context. This view is echoed in the searchlights model which was the underpinning theory of the National Literacy Strategy (2001) in England and Wales.

Many of the strategies used for teaching reading stemming from the psycholinguistic view are still in use in classrooms today and are powerful ways of helping children to become readers. They include: shared reading, guided reading, reading aloud to children, responding to texts and the importance of choosing quality texts. We will see how this works out in practice in some of the following observations.

> **Read**
>
> Meek, M. (1988) *How Texts Teach What Readers Learn*. Stroud: Thimble Press.
>
> Goodman, K. (1992) 'Why whole language is today's agenda in education', *Language Arts*, 69: 354–63.

- In 2006, the Rose Review on early reading was published and moved the underpinning viewpoint in policy-making towards the perspective of cognitive psychology on reading, with a subsequent emphasis on word identification. The first appendix to the Rose Review proposed the 'simple view of reading' (Gough and Tunmer 1986) which distinguishes two elements of reading as word identification and language comprehension.

  The clear distinction between the cognitive psychologists and the psycholinguists is that the former see reading development as a staged process in which there are significant differences between early and experienced readers. Word identification is seen as the key starting point and knowledge of the alphabetic system is central to learning to read. In terms of pedagogical practice, this has led to an emphasis on teaching phonics as the first step in teaching reading. It is argued that systematic phonics teaching should be the first element of a teaching reading programme.

> **Read**
>
> Ehri, L.C. (1995) 'Phases of development in learning to read words by sight', *Journal of Research in Reading*, 18(2): 116–25.

- A third perspective on reading comes from a view that reading is determined by the cultural context in which it takes place. Learning to read happens within a particular situation, and that will determine 'how' reading is; for example, when I read an academic article I read it in a very different way from the way in which I read either a blockbuster novel on the beach or a page on a website from which I am trying to find particular information. I have learned how to read those very different texts for very different purposes because I have belonged to communities who read in those different ways. Some of you will find reading an academic text challenging because it is a new experience and you have never seen anybody doing that and discussed the process with them.

The pedagogical implications of this are important. We need to make sure that we understand what reading experiences the children in our class have had and so what they understand by reading. Many children are not at ease with the print- and narrative-based texts they encounter in school and so struggle because they do not know how to be a reader with these texts. Our starting point for teaching needs to be with texts and experiences that resonate with children's prior experiences.

Read

Heath, S.B. (1983) *Ways with Words*. Cambridge: Cambridge University Press.

Marsh, J. and Millard, E. (2000) *Literacy and Popular Culture: Using Children's Culture in the Classroom*. London: Paul Chapman.

Task

Look at the reading policy in your school. Can you see elements of these three approaches to reading in it? Does one view dominate?

In reality, these three approaches and others are not mutually exclusive, and you are likely to see elements of them all in classrooms. Teachers will use their knowledge of each child and their understanding of the reading process to use the most appropriate approach for the particular time and the particular child.

OBSERVATION: Shared reading in a Reception class (ages 4 and 5)

The children were sitting on the carpet facing the teacher who was sitting on a very low armchair. A visualiser was on a low table next to her and the book was on this and so being shown on the screen in front of the children. A visualiser is a digital camera on an arm which enables the whole class to see a book or an object on a screen. It is an extremely useful teaching tool for shared reading. The book the class was reading together was *The Whale's Song* by Dyan Sheldon and Gary Blythe. It would be helpful if you had a copy of this book with you while you are reading this observation. It is a well-loved text and could be used in Key Stage 2 as effectively as in this Reception class.

The teacher read the title to the class and then asked them, 'Do we normally think of whales singing?'

Comment

By immediately posing a question the teacher actively involves the children in the reading. She is showing them that it is part of being a reader to question what is in a book and to relate your own experiences and current knowledge to the text. The different responses to the question were all listened to and accepted. She did not indicate any answer was correct or wrong but took all as valid points of view.

The teacher then looked at the front cover. She pointed to the words and read the title again and the names of the author and illustrator. She then asked, 'From the front cover, tell the person next to you what sort of book this is.'

Comment

The teacher is using a strategy called 'pair talk'. You might well have experienced this strategy during a training session yourself. It enables children to try out ideas in a safer context than the whole group and encourages more exploratory talk (Bruner 1966). As these were very young children the task was very focused and was developed by the teacher in the feedback time. How do you think it might be different with older children?

After a minute or two, the teacher asked one child for his idea and then said, 'Put your hand up if you agree with Matthew'. Most of the children put up their hands. The teacher then showed the class a 'big book' that they had been reading the previous week. This was a non-fiction text. Very quickly she looked at the book with the children, reminding them of the contents page, the index and the title, and drawing their attention to the characteristics which showed it was non-fiction. She then focused their attention back to *The*

Whale's Song, saying, 'This is a story book. The author is Dyan Sheldon and the illustrator is Gary Blythe'.

She turned to the opening pages and together she and the children looked at the pictures. She introduced them by saying, 'These give us a little taste. They put us in the mood for the story. How do they make you feel?' The children shared the emotions that were evoked by the pictures and were very perceptive and sensitive in the suggestions they made.

Comment

In starting with an affective response to the text, the teacher was demonstrating the importance of personal response. She did not make an evaluative comment on children's responses but accepted them all; she acknowledged the differences and in her acceptance showed that it is expected that there would be different responses to a text.

She then read the first few pages of the book to the children. She pointed with a stick along the text as she read and used her hands to support the meaning of the words.

Comment

Pointing to the written text as you read aloud shows very young children the relationship that there is between the written symbols on the page and the words that are spoken. It also shows them the direction in which English print is read – left to right and top to bottom. Many children will have learned this from their experiences of being read to at home but many more children will not know this. It is something that needs to be learned and for some children it needs to be explicitly taught. It is also important to remember that for some children their experiences of print will be very different – the texts they know are not read from left to right and top to bottom. In pointing to the text smoothly underneath the print rather than pointing to each separate word in turn, the teacher was showing the importance of fluent phrased reading rather than word-by-word reading. The use of actions to support the meaning of the words makes it accessible to more children, especially those who have English as an additional language.

Attention was then turned to the illustration, which shows Lily sitting on her grandmother's lap looking up into her face. The teacher asked the children what was happening in the picture and there was a general response that

Lily was listening to her grandmother. She then said, 'Could you make me a face like Lily's face – when you're really interested in what somebody's telling you?'

> **Comment**
> Through asking the children to imitate the expressions in the picture, the children were helped to identify with and so empathise with the character, Lily. The act of physically making a facial expression made concrete an abstract emotion and also focused their thinking on the fact that Lily's grandmother was telling a story to Lily, but also to them.

The teacher then went on to read the story to the children. As the shared reading continued the teacher occasionally stopped to ask the children to talk about or respond to something. 'Talk to the person next to you and tell them what you would give them as the perfect present.' Sometimes she pointed out a word for the children to identify. 'There's a word on this page that you recognise. Can you see? There look, it says 'whales'.

There were times when the children interrupted to ask questions. 'What does silent mean?' The teacher responded, 'I'm glad you asked that question. It means it is very quiet – no sound can be heard.'

> **Comment**
> Notice how positively the teacher responds to the child's question. She first is pleased that the question is asked and then she answers it clearly and briefly. This response shows that it was a sensible and important question to ask because without understanding this word some of the meaning of the whole text might be lost. In this case however, the teacher wanted to establish the meaning of the word quickly so that she could get on with reading the story. She made a professional judgement about a way of responding that best suited the purpose of the lesson.

When the story came to an end there was a short moment of silence while the children absorbed and thought about what they had heard. It is important to allow these moments of reflection where children are relating new knowledge to prior experiences and understanding.

Jessica then asked, 'Is it real?' the teacher responded, 'It could be real Jessica – a real dream. It wasn't a dream for Lily. In stories anything can happen.'

Comment

This is an interesting exchange between Jessica and the teacher, where the teacher is teaching about the characteristics of fiction. Remember how at the start of this observation she reminded the children of a non-fiction text they had been reading. After reading this very poetic imaginary tale she is highlighting the differences between the two text types and recognising them both as valid but different reading experiences.

After finishing the discussion on the content of the book and on the children's affective responses to it, the teacher then asked, 'What helped me to read this story to you?' The answer given by several children was, 'The words.' The teacher then asked, 'Did I just make the words up?' After loud responses in the negative from the class, the teacher commented, 'No, I didn't and later on we're going to do some work on sounds to show us how the sounds can help us to read the words'.

Comment

The class had read and responded to this wonderful book. They had talked about the ideas and feelings it had evoked and had related it to their own experiences, knowledge and understandings. The teacher then went on to put the phonics teaching into the real and relevant context of reading and to make explicit to them the purpose for learning about phoneme and grapheme correspondences. Many years ago Halliday (1976) wrote that those who are the most successful literacy learners are those who understand the purposes of literacy. Consider how the children in this class are being introduced to some of the purposes of literacy. Note especially that this is being made absolutely explicit to them – never assume that children will just pick things up!

The observation above is a good example of the way in which children need to be taught about what it means to be a reader as well as the mechanical skills of reading. As a reader the most important part is to understand what the author has said and to respond to that, drawing on your own knowledge, experiences and understanding. That process was being modelled to the children in the shared reading lesson. Towards the end of the lesson, however, the teacher reminded them that in order to be able to read independently they need to be able to decode the words. That is done through phonics – learning the relationship between the phonemes and the graphemes. Phonics is an important element in the teaching of reading for very young children.

In phonic teaching children are learning about the phonemes (sounds) of language and how they are written down by using graphemes. English is an alphabetic language. There are about 44 different phonemes in the English language and they are represented by graphemes. Each sound is represented by one grapheme. It would be simple if we had 44 sounds and 44 letters to represent them – life would be much easier! You know, however, that there are only 26 letters in the English alphabet and so some graphemes consist of two or more letters, for example, /th/ and /sh/. This is not straightforward and children need explicit and systematic teaching to enable them to segment (break a word down into its sounds to write) and blend (build the sounds together into words to read). The next two observations focus on phonic teaching.

OBSERVATION: Phonic teaching in a Reception class (ages 4 and 5)

In this class, phonic teaching is systematic and teaching is done each day, followed up by activities within the free-flow time. Each phoneme–grapheme correspondence is taught to the whole group with a multi-sensory approach. The initial sound/shape of the grapheme is taught by whole group input as a story or song, involving all the children in listening, speaking, writing the grapheme in the air and/or on the carpet before beginning more targeted phonics activities. For the rest of the session, available activities within the foundation unit will be mainly supporting the phonics input and a recap at the end of the session will remind the children of what they have learned that day.

Before the group session, objects had been hidden around the unit which the children discovered and identified with an adult. Many of them had worked out the initial phoneme and were able to answer the first question of the session, 'Which sound do you think we might be learning about today?'

> **Comment**
> The prior learning activity gave children ownership of the learning. They were able to problem-solve and work out the focus of the activity and so felt in control and confident because they had already achieved even before the lesson had begun.

The observed session focused on /t/. The children were told a story by the teacher about going on a picnic and hearing strange sounds from a nearby field. When the teacher went to investigate, she could hear the sounds 't –t-t-t' getting louder and louder. She discovered in a field some teeny tiny teddies playing tennis; every time they hit the ball, it made the sound /t/. All the other teddies were watching them, turning their heads from side to side to watch the tennis ball. The teacher and teaching assistant role-played this with tennis raquets and foam balls, while the children sat in a circle around the edge of the carpet, turning their heads and saying /t/ every time the ball was hit.

Comment

The teaching was contextualised within a story. We all make sense of our experiences by telling stories and by placing new learning within a story. The teacher was providing a hook on which the children could hang the new learning. Anne Haas Dyson has written much about how young children learn about the symbolic power of literacy through their play. In the worlds children create in play, they are sharing and creating interpretations of their experiences. The story puts the representation of reality into a concrete context and as Dyson says, 'enacted symbolic worlds are given more permanent and visual casings' (1993: 4). The abstract sound 't' was put into a story and this enabled the children to remember and understand the symbolic representation which might otherwise be too abstract and remote from their realities.

Read

Dyson, A.H. (1993) *The Social Worlds of Children Learning to Write in an Urban Primary School*. New York: Teachers College Press.

The shape of the letter was introduced with the song, 'down, around, off and across', sung by the teacher while she wrote the grapheme in the air. After a few times the children joined in, singing while drawing the letter in the air. They then sang together a song:

Teddies playing tennis, t-t-t
Teddies playing tennis, t-t-t
Teddies playing tennis, t-t-t
Now I know my letter 'tee'

Comment

Rhymes and songs were central elements of the lesson. They enabled the children both to practise and to remind themselves of what they had learned.

Figure 3.1 Discrete phonic teaching with 4- and 5-year-olds

During the rest of the session the children wrote a recipe for tomato puree (adult led) to practise letter formation, had a teddies' tea party with triangles of toast and teacakes, had a teeny tiny 't' painted on their tiniest toe and went outside for a number hunt for 10 tiny teddies. The rest of the unit was resourced appropriately for free choice activities but with tractors and trailers in the sand, torn tissue to make a town in the art area, tigers and turtles in the lentil tray and tea bags in the water tray.

Comment

Look carefully at all the follow-up activities which were planned for the rest of the session. What is essential to ensure that they are successful as strategies for reinforcing the direct phonic teaching? Children may play with tractors and trailers, tear up tissue paper to make a town, squeeze teabags in the water, hunt for tiny teddies and find turtles and tigers in the lentils but, unless an adult talks with them about this in a way that focuses their attention on the phoneme, those activities will not support the direct phonic teaching. When planning, adults need to be primed that this is the focus so that in their talk and questioning they are emphasising the phoneme all the time and encouraging the children to articulate it.

Task

List some of the things you might plan to say to the children during these activities. What questions would you ask in a review time to focus on the learning of the phoneme?

This lesson clearly matches one of the criteria given for effective phonics teaching – 'use a multi-sensory approach so that children learn variously from simultaneous visual, auditory and kinaesthetic activities which are designed to secure essential phonic knowledge and skills' (www.education.gov.uk/schools/teachingand learning/pedagogy/teachingstyles/phonics/a0010240/criteria-for-assuring-high-quality-phonic-work). This website is no longer active but the principle of a multi-sensory approach to teaching remains firm and relates to much of what we know about how children learn. Research identifies some central points that should be borne in mind when planning teaching. Jane Medwell and others did some research which identified the characteristics of effective teachers of literacy (Wray et al. 2000). When talking about phonic teaching, these were:

- phonics taught within the context of a text
- teacher modelling how the sound works
- explicit connections made between the sound and the symbol
- lessons having a brisk pace
- short regular phonic sessions
- explicit teaching reflected in the classroom environment.

Read

Wray, D., Medwell, J., Fox, R. and Poulson, L. (2000) 'The teaching practices of effective teachers of literacy', *Educational Review*, 52(1): 75–84.

Task

Match these characteristics of effective teaching to this observation and other observations you make in your own class.

Summary: Reading in the reception class

We have looked at two observations from reception classes and have seen how the different aspects of the reading process are explicitly taught to the children. In the first observation the children were being shown how to behave as readers, they were encouraged to make a personal response to the text and to share these responses with each other. They were encouraged to ask questions and to relate what they were reading to their own understandings. In this lesson they were being taught how to behave as readers.

In the second observation they were learning the decoding skills necessary to read independently. The teaching involved them and conveyed the same knowledge and skills in a variety of multi-sensual ways. They were having fun and had lots of opportunities to practise their new learning in different contexts.

It was clear in both observations that talk is a key element in a successful learning activity; children need opportunities to articulate their learning and to explore for themselves with others new ideas and concepts. The skilled teacher supports them in this through scaffolding and sensitive questioning. We will see more examples of this later on – but when observing look at the questions teachers ask and consider how they support and challenge.

OBSERVATION: Phonic teaching with a group of Year 1 children (ages 5 and 6)

Tables were set out in the classroom in a semi-circle with a magnetic board and a box of magnetic letters set out on each table – enough for one between two. As the group of eight children (five boys and three girls) came into the room they sat on the floor in a semicircle in front of the teacher who sat on a chair.

> **Comment**
> The room is prepared for the lesson with the magnetic boards set out and boxes with the appropriate magnetic letters in them next to the boards. This means that valuable teaching time is not wasted by getting resources out.

The teacher quickly showed the children cards with graphemes on and asked them to say the phoneme represented by the grapheme. This is a revision exercise of prior learning and most were clearly recognised.

> **Comment**
> This was done very quickly. The children were clearly familiar with most of these phoneme–grapheme correspondences and time is only spent on those which have been introduced recently.

The card shown is /ai/. A child responds with /a/. The teacher replies, 'It would be /a/ but it has a letter "i" next to it and so it is an /ā/'.

Sometimes the teacher prompts by reminding the children of the action that accompanies the sound.

> **Comment**
> Here the teacher is relating to all learning styles and making the taught concept very clear. She gives a reason why the answer given was wrong but in her reason shows that it was a reasonable response to have made. She then explains why it was wrong and the symbols that also need to be taken into account. When children have begun by learning graphemes which contain just a single letter, it can be confusing when they progress to graphemes that consist of two or more letters. Including the action will support the kinaesthetic learners. Some children will remember by action, some by looking at the picture and some by the sound and/or the contextualising story. All aspects need to be included in a lesson.

As this part of the lesson comes to an end, the teacher says, 'There are three cards left: /air/, /ear/ and /ure/. Who can come and show me which one says /air/?'

> **Comment**
> The children are given the choice so that nobody is put on the spot. The way the question is framed means that most of the children were looking to see if they could rise to the challenge.

A child comes up to the front and points to the card which says /ear/. He then changes his mind and points to /air/. The teacher asks, 'Why did you change your mind?'

> **Comment**
> The child clearly felt confident to change his mind. It is important that this is the case in classrooms; we learn by making mistakes and talking about them. The teacher asks the child to talk through his decision-making process. It is being able to explain something to somebody else that indicates real learning. It also allows the teacher to gauge his understanding and use this for further teaching.

The child replies, 'Because it's got an "a" in it.'

> **Comment**
> This child is clearly making a visual distinction between the words rather than focusing on the representation of the phoneme. It may be that the letter 'a' acts as a mnemonic for the child. The teacher might want to note this and see if the child can recognise this grapheme on other occasions.

The lesson then moves on to the next phase. The teacher says, 'I wonder if you've been practising your spellings. Let's sound them out.' She holds up a card with the word 'bent' written on it. The children sound out the word phoneme by phoneme and then do the same with 'sent'.

Comment
The children are here practising segmenting with simple phonically regular words. Note the relationship between segmentation (breaking words into sounds) and blending (building sounds into words). Both skills are needed for reading and writing.

The teacher then holds up both cards and asks how the two words are similar. One child replies that they both have 'ent' in them.

Comment
The children have sounded out these words and the teacher is wanting them to recognise them by sight. Ehri (1995) believed that when beginner readers are faced with an unfamiliar word, the ability to phonologically recode the word provides an access route for the visual into the memory. In simple terms, that means that learning the sound–symbol correspondence helps the visual to 'stick' in the memory more effectively than relying on just the visual pattern of the word.

The teacher replies, 'Well done! The "ent" is the same but the first sound is different. We're going to look at the first sounds a bit more. On the tables with the magnetic letters I want you to make "bent". Then we're going to change it to "went" and then we're going to see if we can think of rhyming words.'

Comment
The children are here working on the onset and rime of words. The onset is the sound before the first vowel and the rime is the rest of the word. Monosyllabic words (words with only one syllable) can be changed by putting a new onset on the rime to create new words. If a word has more than one syllable then the same principle applies to each syllable. This exercise is helping children to create new words from words already known. This can be described as using analogy. To complete this task the children are required to both look at the visual pattern and say the sound of the word. Working with these larger chunks of sound can be more supportive for children who struggle with phoneme identification.

The children move to the tables and sit in pairs. They clearly have fixed places in which to sit and working pairs are already established so the transition occurs smoothly. The teacher says, 'First, we're going to make "bent". Tip out the letters to make it easier'. She walks around the tables, checking and commenting to individual children. 'Is that a "b"? No – it's a "d". Can you find me one that is the right way round?'

> ### Comment
> Many children of this age confuse 'b' and 'd' and it is not an indication of significant difficulties unless they carry on doing it when they are more experienced readers and writers. Learning the orientation of letters is challenging for some children; when learning to name objects the orientation does not matter but it is highly significant when naming letters. Remember that confusion can also be aural ('k' and 'g') as well as visual.

To another child the teacher says, 'What comes next? Say the word slowly to me. Think about what the next sound is. So – what letter are you looking for?'

> ### Comment
> The teacher is encouraging the child to listen to the sounds and segment the word. If this is done orally first, it is easier to identify the grapheme which represents the phoneme. Relate this back to Ehri's theory which was discussed earlier.

'You've made them. Good! Now look at the "-ent". Take the first letters away. See if you can put another letter in to make a different word. Just try the letters and see if they make real words.'

> ### Comment
> The physical manipulation of the magnetic letters helps young children to understand what it is they are doing. It is easier to move and change magnetic letters than to write them down on paper. Note also how the children are encouraged to say the words.

'"Shent" – that's an interesting word. What does it mean? /sh/ is a sound. It's a rhyming word but it's not a real word.'

> ### Comment
> The teacher accepts a nonsense word because the child has done exactly what was required – changed the onset while retaining the same rime.

'Brilliant! "Sent" – I sent a letter.'

Comment

By putting the word into a sentence the teacher is clarifying the meaning and establishing comprehension as the prime purpose of both reading and writing.

'That's good. But "gent" is a very silly word. It doesn't start with "j" but "g"'.

Comment

The teacher accepts the word as the child has fulfilled the required task. However, she explains simply that some words do not conform to expectations. Her use of the phrase 'silly word' shows the child that she has not made a mistake it is just that the conventional spelling is unexpected.

Note what the teacher needed to know in order to teach phonics effectively. First, she had secure knowledge about how the alphabet works. She knew the phonemes and their corresponding graphemes. She does not use the technical terms in her teaching but you will see many teachers who do. It can certainly be less confusing to use the term 'grapheme' when referring to phonemes written down. A grapheme is a letter or group of letters representing one sound.

A teacher needs to be confident in phonic knowledge in order to address the children's misconceptions. This teacher needed to know different graphemic representations of the same phoneme and she needed to know what a child was doing when he identified a grapheme. She needed to have a language for talking about the sounds, letters and words which is both accurate, clear and able to be understood by the children. She also needed to know about how the sounds are produced (phonetics) and which sounds are so similar that confusion can arise between for example voiced and unvoiced sounds (/p/ and /b/, /t/ and /d/, /k/ and /g/).

In this lesson the teacher is using a mixture of synthetic and analytic phonics. **Synthetic phonics** is when children are taught to read by identifying the phonemes represented by particular graphemes. The phonemes are then blended to create a word. The children were doing this when they were reading the words on the flashcards by 'sounding them out'. When they were writing the words by using the magnetic letters, the children were segmenting the words by splitting them up into phonemes and representing them by particular graphemes.

Analytic phonemes is when children analyse patterns in words and identify the graphemes which represent those patterns. The children here were looking at the pattern '-ent' which was common to all the words. This is the rime of the word and by changing the onset they were creating different words by the use of analogy. They used their knowledge of the words 'bent' and 'went' to create new words ending in '-ent'.

It is highly unlikely that you will encounter a teacher of early reading who does not pay close attention to the alphabetic nature of print in English. In the early twenty-first century, teachers are encouraged to rely on systematic synthetic phonics as their main approach. You might like to read some of the debate around this and decide for yourself the best way of helping young children understand the world of print. You might well discover that different ways work best with different children!

Read

Johnston, R. and Watson, J. (2007) *Teaching Synthetic Phonics*. Exeter: Learning Matters.

Wyse, D. and Styles, M. (2007) 'Synthetic phonics and the teaching of reading: the debate surrounding England's "Rose Report"', *Literacy*, 47(1): 35–42.

Goouch, K. and Lambirth, A. (2008) *Understanding Phonics and the Teaching of Reading: Critical Perspectives*. Maidenhead: McGraw-Hill/Open University Press.

The lesson above was clearly part of a systematic programme of phonic teaching. When you are observing in school, ask to see the medium-term or unit plans from which an individual lesson comes. You should be able to trace the development of phonic knowledge and relate what was going on in the observed lesson to the stages of development. Try and look at a copy of *Letters and Sounds* (DfES 2007) which will describe six stages of development in phonic teaching with lots of practical ideas for games and activities.

This lesson was a discrete daily session and the children were progressing from simple to more complex phonic knowledge and skills, and covering one of the major grapheme–phoneme correspondences. The lesson was taught in a small group and the teacher was monitoring understanding continually throughout the lesson. When you observe a lesson, talk with the teacher afterwards about how she or he records the learning achieved and how that prior learning is built upon in subsequent lessons.

The lesson used a variety of teaching and learning strategies. The children were involved in reading and spelling words, in making up new words orally, in manipulating magnetic letters to spell known words and make up new words and working as a member of a group, in a pair and individually. Effective phonic teaching consists of multi-sensory activities that are 'interesting and engaging but firmly focused on intensifying the learning associated with its phonic goal' (www.education.gov.uk/schools/teaching/pedagogy/teachingstyles/phonics/a0010240/criteria-for-assuring-high-quality-phonic-work).

> **Task**
> Draw up a list of multi-sensory strategies that you observe and include them in your own lesson planning. Remember though that they should be simple and quick and have a very clear focus.

There was a clear sense of progression within this lesson. It began with a recap of previous knowledge, moving quickly through those phoneme–grapheme correspondences which were learned previously and spending more time on those learned recently. The teacher followed up on children's comments and attempts at word creation and used these as teaching points. Note how she took the three graphemes with which the children struggled, and focused on those for a short teaching interaction. She questioned the children, asking them to explain their thinking and so extending their understanding and strengthening the learning.

In a written account of a lesson it is difficult to convey the enthusiasm of both teacher and children and to show how the teacher related to the children. There are some clues in the language she used: '"gent" is a very silly word'; 'just try the letters and see'; 'that is an interesting word'. In her responses to the children the teacher always took them completely seriously. She respected and valued their contributions and took even their mistakes as serious attempts and responded accordingly. She knew the children well enough to know what they would find amusing, interesting or exciting and she herself was amused, interested and excited with them. In short, she saw the activity through the eyes of 5-year-old children and joined with them in the problem-solving they were engaged in. It is when the teacher works alongside the children as co-learner that an ethos of enquiry is created. Look for examples of this in lessons you observe.

Shared reading

The first observation in this chapter was of shared reading in a reception class. Shared reading is a reading lesson with the whole class using either a big book, a visualiser or an e-book on screen. The purpose of shared reading is to teach explicitly reading strategies. In the observed lesson the children were being taught about comprehension – they were learning how to predict and to empathise, to construct images and to question the text, to explore how the author created effects and to respond emotionally to the text. Towards the end of the text they were also taught about the relationship between the written and spoken language. The teacher was using a text which the children would not have been able to read independently and was teaching reading strategies through modelling and questioning.

Guided reading

Guided reading is a reading lesson with a small group of approximately six children, usually of roughly the same reading ability, using a text which the children can read independently with support. In guided reading the children are 'guided' to use independently the reading strategies they have been taught previously and are supported or scaffolded in this by the teacher. The scaffolding may take the form of the nature of the activity or the type of talk; scaffolding is how the teacher supports the independent work of the children.

Read
Pentimonti, J.M. and Justice, L.M. (2010) 'Teachers' use of scaffolding strategies during read alouds in the preschool classroom', *Early Childhood Education Journal*, 37(4): 241–8.

Verenikina, I. (2004) 'From theory to practice: what does the metaphor of scaffolding mean to educators today?', *Outlines: Critical Practice Studies*, no. 2.

OBSERVATION: Guided reading in Year 2 (ages 6 and 7)

Six children are sitting around a table with the class teacher. The rest of the class is engaged in independent reading activities – browsing in the book corner, writing reviews or spotting adjectives in a text.

The teacher starts by informing the children of the learning objective of the lesson, which is 'to be able to recognise adjectives and understand they add detail and interest to stories'. The teacher then asked the children to explain to a partner what they thought an adjective was.

Comment
Understanding grammatical terms is best done in the context of understanding what a word does in a sentence. It might be better to have asked the children what adjectives do and to stress how adjectives tell us more as readers. Adjectives help us to create pictures of characters or settings. For example, 'a tall thin grumpy-faced man' tells us more about the character in a story than just 'a man'.

The three pairs then shared their ideas about adjectives and the teacher emphasised the point that adjectives make stories more interesting. The big book *Stellaluna* (Cannon, 1993) was then introduced to the children. The children had been read this book before in a read-aloud session and had discussed the power and poignancy of the story. They had responded to the book personally and had talked about the story and the different characters. This guided reading session was to explore how the author created those effects on readers that they had previously experienced.

The teacher read the first three or four pages to the group. Each child had a whiteboard and a pen and they were asked to write down some of the adjectives they heard on their boards. After the reading these words were shared.

Comment

By giving the children a specific task to do while listening to the reading, the teacher was focusing their listening and ensuring that they were engaged in active listening. They were not under pressure to record all the adjectives and the careful instructions meant that the children were not under pressure. The way in which the adjectives were shared created an atmosphere of collaboration – the children were really working together to identify the adjectives.

When the adjectives had been listed, the teacher reread the extract leaving all the adjectives out. The group then discussed their response to this as a reader and the effect the adjectives had on their understanding of the story.

Comment

The whole focus was on reading the text to see how the writer had used words to create particular effects. This is an important strategy called 'reading like a writer' and demonstrates the inextricable links between reading and writing. Children cannot be expected to write brilliant, exciting and imaginative stories if they have not read stories like that and perhaps more importantly also talked about what makes those stories brilliant, exciting and imaginative.

Read

Barrs, M. and Cork, V. (2002) *The Reader in the Writer.* London: CLPE.

The children were then given a copy of a short story called 'Brave Together', written by the teacher, and asked to read it in pairs. Before they began reading they were reminded of the different strategies they could use to help work out words they do not know – use the clues in the picture, use their phonic skills to blend the phonemes to make a word, read ahead for the meaning, leave the word out, go back and start the sentence again, and so on.

Comment

One of the important elements of a guided reading lesson is what is often called a 'strategy check'. This involves reminding the children what they can do to help them work out an unknown word. The main aim of teaching reading is to enable children to read independently, and they will never be able to do that if they do not have strategies to tackle unknown words. It is important that children are given a variety of strategies; there are some words which they will never be able to build up from the sounds and others which they will never be able to work out from the context. Children need a variety of strategies at their disposal. These strategies will be taught explicitly in shared reading and phonic sessions and will be practised and emphasised in guided reading sessions.

The children read the story together, taking it in turns to read aloud in their pairs. This meant that at one time three children were reading aloud at once. The teacher tuned into each of them, listening to what they were doing and supporting as and when necessary.

Comment

This can be a challenging aspect of guided reading. The children read aloud at their own pace at the same time. You will find that the children are able to do this quite easily and are not distracted by each other. As a teacher, you will have to practise tuning your ear in to each child in turn to listen to their reading and to observe the reading strategies they are using. When listening to children read aloud, we need to make sure that their reading is fluent and flowing. We often use the term 'phrased reading'; this means that the words go together appropriately and the reading is not word by word or with pauses in inappropriate places. Listening to how children read texts aloud will often give you an indication of how they are understanding the text.

When the story had been read the teacher led a short discussion on how the adjectives had enriched the story and how the children had responded to them.

Comment

The teacher was continually emphasising that the author had been using language and choosing words in a particular way in order to create a specific response in the readers. Why do you think this is important?

The teacher then brought out a small cuddly dragon toy. After much admiration and discussion, she asked the children to write adjectives on their whiteboard to describe him. They did this very quickly, not worrying about spelling or handwriting. Three children then volunteered to read their sentence to the group. As they read, the rest of the group were encouraged to look very carefully at the dragon to see how these adjectives related to him and how they would help somebody who was not there to get an idea of what the dragon was like. As each adjective was discussed the teacher wrote them on a large luggage label which was then tied round the dragon's neck. Adjectives chosen included green, smiley, friendly, pointy.

> **Comment**
> This time the teacher was using a concrete object as a tool for teaching about adjectives. This meant the children could look at, touch and discuss the dragon, and so think about different words to use. You will see from the list that the children generated that some adjectives relate to the physical observable appearance of the dragon and some are inferential – the children were interpreting what they saw. The whole activity was put in the context of helping somebody who was not there to imagine the dragon – putting into a concrete activity what writers are doing and emphasising the visualisation that many readers do when reading.

The lesson ended by referring back to the learning objective. Each child was given three large coloured and laminated card circles. The red circle would indicate that they did not understand and needed to revisit this topic; the yellow circle indicated that they did understand to a certain degree but needed further work; the green circle indicated that they were confident in what the lesson had covered. The teacher asked the children to hold up a circle – four of them held up green circles and two held up yellow.

> **Comment**
> Asking children to evaluate their own learning is a powerful assessment tool and can be used to inform future planning. You must however be sure that they are evaluating against clear and very specific criteria. This means that learning objectives must be precisely phrased and that all activities within a lesson relate to them. Do you think this was the case in this lesson?

OBSERVATION: Guided reading in Year 5 (ages 9 and 10)

We began the chapter with a focus on teaching comprehension in the Foundation Stage and we close with an observation of comprehension in the upper end of Key Stage 2. The observation is part of a unit of work and we will return to another lesson in this unit in the next chapter on writing.

With older children there tends to be less emphasis on practising reading strategies for decoding, and so children will be reading silently or will have read a passage before the lesson and during the lesson they will be discussing their different types of responses to the text. For the observed lesson the children had read part of chapter 8 of *Oliver Twist* by Charles Dickens. Although they had read it to themselves before the lesson, the teacher read the extract aloud to them at the start.

Comment

This was a challenging text for these children. In the previous lesson with the whole class the teacher had compared a passage from a book by Roald Dahl with a passage from Dickens. They had discussed the types of language used and the vocabulary. This provided the children with a good starting point. However, they still needed the mediation of the teacher reading aloud to them to help them to fully access the meaning of the text.

The teacher began by asking the question, 'What did Fagin look like?' This was a question which could be answered by direct referral to the text. It is what is known as a 'literal' question. The children did not need to interpret; they just had to read and identify the relevant information from the text. There was some discussion about this and a list of words and phrases were written on the whiteboard describing Fagin.

The next question was, 'What did Oliver find frightening?' This was a slightly different type of question because it required the children to infer from the text. The teacher required the children to quote from the text to say why they said what they did. Every comment was accepted as long as some justification was given. Inferring information from the text is the next level of comprehension. It could be described as 'reading between the lines'.

In this lesson the teacher did not progress to ask an evaluative or application question, which would see if the children could apply the understanding of the text to another context.

Comment

There are different levels of comprehension and in planning conversations around texts teachers need to be aware of and plan for all of these:

* **Literal comprehension** questions centre on ideas and information that are explicit in a text. They require the recognition or recall of a fact or facts.

For example, what was the name of John's dog?

- **Inferential comprehension** questions require children to 'read between the lines'. For example, how did John's mum feel about the dog?
- **Deductive comprehension** questions require children to dig deeper into the text. They need to make inferences based on the text and also draw on their own experience and knowledge, thinking about cause and effect. For example, describe how John felt at the end of the story.
- **Evaluative comprehension** questions ask for an evaluation of arguments or ideas suggested by the text. Readers have to compare the information provided with their own experiences, knowledge or values. For example, was John's dad right in what he said about the dog?

Summary

The teaching of reading takes many forms and cannot be limited either to short lessons or to hearing children read from particular types of books. In 2003 the International Academy of Education published a paper on teaching reading in which they said,

> Both research and classroom practices support the use of a balanced approach in instruction. Because reading depends on efficient word recognition and comprehension, instruction should develop reading skills and strategies, as well as build on learners' knowledge through the use of authentic texts.
>
> Teaching reading and writing is difficult work. Teachers must be aware of the progress that students are making and adjust instruction to the changing abilities of students. It is also important to remember that the goal of reading is to understand the texts and to be able to learn from them. (Pang et al., 2003: 7, 21)

Think carefully about these statements and consider what you will do in your classroom to achieve these aims and help your pupils to become enthusiastic and critical readers.

Further reading

Flynn, N. and Stainthorp, R. (2006) *The Learning and Teaching of Reading and Writing*. Oxford: Wiley Blackwell.

Graham, J. and Kelly, A. (2007) *Reading Under Control: Teaching Reading in the Primary School*. 3rd edn. London: David Fulton.

CHAPTER 4

TEACHING WRITING

Teaching reading and teaching writing are inextricably linked and both are surrounded by talk. This chapter focuses on teaching writing, one of the most challenging tasks for any teacher. The observations look at the process of writing and explore ways in which teachers have made this explicit to children.

Writing is one of the most difficult activities we engage in – I can vouch for that as I sit in front of my computer writing this! You will know how difficult it is when you try to write an assignment or a difficult email or clear instructions for a stranger. It is difficult because it lacks all the elements of spoken language which help us to know that our message is understood – the facial and verbal expressions of the listener, the interruptions and questions, the chance to rephrase and repeat ourselves and the context in which the message is spoken. In writing, the reader is absent, there are no opportunities to have a second go and there are many ways in which a written message can be misinterpreted. These are all reasons why written language needs to be clear and unambiguous – a challenging aim.

When we teach young children it helps to keep five key words in mind.

Composition

This is the process of authoring a text – of sorting out ideas and deciding on the best way of expressing them, of structuring thoughts and making them accessible to others and of expressing what you imagine and dream to others. Composing a text does not have to be done in front of a computer or with a pencil in your hand. As I have been writing this book I have spent a lot of time wandering around the house, making coffee, tidying up and sometimes even doing the ironing! While doing all these things, though, I have been rather distracted and have not wanted to talk to anybody or to read or watch television. That is because I have been composing the text in my head; I have been trying out different ways of expressing what I want to communicate and working out in what order things should be written. When I actually come to the computer I have a fair idea of what I want to say, although many changes are continually made.

It is important that children learning to be writers realise that this is what writing is like. It is about having something to say and working out how best to say it – it is about composing a text. The teaching strategy of shared writing is a way of making this explicit to children and we will consider an example of that later.

Transcription

Once a writer has had an idea and knows how she wants to express it, she then has to pick up a pencil or switch on the keyboard. She needs to know how to form letters or to use a keyboard and how to spell, punctuate and construct grammatically clear sentences. These are important skills and need to be taught and learned. However, I can compose a text and be an author without ever using transcriptional skills – I can dictate my composition to a scribe or use voice-activated software. Very young children can compose texts – they do not have to wait until they have sufficiently competent transcriptional skills. They can dictate their writing to an adult or older child or they can record it using emergent writing.

These two skills, composition and transcription, need to be taught and learned alongside each other. It is no good having brilliant ideas if you are not able to record them for other people to read, and it is no good having neat handwriting, perfect spelling, punctuation and grammar, if you have nothing to say!

Purpose, audience and format

The next three words work together. Imagine I want to leave a note to my son to ask him to put the wheelie bins at the end of the drive before he goes to school. I am likely to find a scrap of paper and a pen and write, 'Don't forget wheelie bins'. He will know, from prior experience, what that means and will work out that it is from one of his parents. He would be very surprised if I wrote a formal letter on the computer and posted it to him. However, if I wanted to make a complaint to the manager of a shop, it is not likely to have much effect if I stick a note on his door saying, 'TV doesn't work'. He would not know who it was from and would be likely to put the note in the bin with no action.

As a writer, I decide on the purpose of my writing and the audience of my writing and that will determine the format of my writing – the style and layout and use of language. Young children need to be able to make those decisions appropriately.

One of the most influential researchers on the teaching of writing has been Donald Graves. He stressed the importance of seeing writing as a process in which we plan, draft, edit and revise our writing. His thinking has had much impact on pedagogical practice and recent research confirms his view. Andrews et al. (2009) argued that effective teaching of writing includes a model of the writing process in which planning, drafting, editing and revision are a central part.

Read

Graves, D.H. (1983) *Writing: Teachers and Children at Work*. Portsmouth, NH: Heinemann Educational.

Andrews, R., Torgerson, C., Low, G. and McGuinn, N. (2009) 'Teaching argument writing to 7–14 year olds: an international review of the evidence of successful practice', *Cambridge Journal of Education*, 39(3): 291–310.

OBSERVATION: Composition in Year 4 (ages 8 and 9)

In the following observation of writing with 8- and 9-year-olds look for evidence of the writing process at work. How are the children being encouraged to plan and draft their writing? You might also want to consider the place of editing and revision. Do you think this needs to happen with everything a pupil writes? How would you justify your answer?

The class were looking at persuasive writing and the work was based on the text, *Click, Clack, Moo, Cows that Type* by Dorothy Cronin. The teacher read the first few pages of the text, finishing up with the large illustration showing Farmer Brown looking very cross, grumpy and rather puzzled.

The children then spent time in groups working out how Farmer Brown was feeling, what he might be thinking and why. They were encouraged to make suggestions, backing them up by reference to the text.

Comment

This activity allowed the children to 'get into the mind' of Farmer Brown. They were putting themselves in his place and by empathising with him were able to consider his emotions and feelings. It also required them to infer things from the text – both the written text and the illustrations. This 'reading between and beyond' the lines is an important skill for readers to develop. Sharing and justifying their ideas in a group also meant that the children were thinking carefully about what they said. They were willing to challenge each other and to debate different viewpoints.

The ideas generated in the groups were fed back as a whole group and recorded on the whiteboard. As each point was made by a child, the teacher required them to justify it and refer back to the text for support.

The children were then set the task of writing a letter from the cows to Farmer Brown. This was done as a shared writing activity in their small groups. The children made suggestions as to what was written, discussed it among themselves, came to a consensus and it was recorded on a large sheet of paper in felt pen. Throughout this process the children were continually rereading what had already been written and checking that this was what the group meant to say. Halfway through the lesson the teacher stopped the class and asked each group to read out what they had written so far. She asked for comments from other groups and checked with the writers that they were happy and knew what they wanted to say next. The writing contained many crossings out and arrows moving phrases and words around. Once it was completed the whole text was read to check that the group was happy with it.

Comment

Shared writing is a strategy which makes explicit all the thinking that normally goes on in the head of a writer. It can take one of three forms: demonstration, teacher scribing and supported composition. Demonstration is when the teacher writes in front of the class and makes a running commentary on the whole writing process; she would articulate the decisions she made, try out sentences before she wrote them and change things she was not happy with. Teacher scribing is when the children compose a text and the teacher acts as scribe, writing it down on a flip chart or whiteboard.

This is a useful way for the teacher to model the revising and editing process, showing the children the sort of things they might ask themselves when they are writing.

The example of shared writing in this observation is of supported composition; the children were in Year 5 and it can be assumed that they would have had a lot of experience of the other types of shared writing activity. The children were working together to compose and transcribe and so had to discuss the decisions that writers have to make. The teacher was supporting them in this reflective process and the teaching assistant was acting as scribe for one group.

Task

Observe some shared writing sessions and decide whether it is demonstration, teacher scribing or supported composition. After the observation, think about the respective roles of teacher and children and how they change in the different activities.

This activity allowed the children to empathise with Farmer Brown and understand his reactions and feelings. In the following lesson attention was then turned to the cows! In the book the cows hold a meeting behind the closed doors of the shed to discuss their response to Farmer Brown's initiative. The children became the cows and held their meeting. Before the meeting each child was asked to make notes on what they thought and how they felt the cows should respond to Farmer Brown. Feelings were shared and different viewpoints of an appropriate response were hotly discussed. The children were required to explain and fully justify their views and the group had to come to a consensus after hearing different perspectives. Once this had been reached, each group was required to write a report of their meeting showing how they had reached the consensus. One member of the group was appointed as scribe and the teacher and teaching assistant worked with those children who needed more support. This writing activity followed a very similar pattern to the previous shared writing activity. The more able children were challenged by doing the writing with less scaffolding than previously. Those who needed support were given it and their writing was a guided writing time.

> **Comment**
> Guided writing is very similar to guided reading in that it allows a teacher to provide structured and focused support to a group of children who have similar needs at a particular stage of the writing process. In this situation the teacher worked with a group of children who needed help in sorting out their ideas and recording them in a way which was meaningful for the reader. The teacher acted as scribe and the children composed the text, using the strategy of 'oral composition' to try out their ideas. The teaching assistant worked with a group who needed support in working as a group and was there to model and demonstrate collaborative working – ensuring that everybody's voice was heard and that everybody made a contribution to the final product.

Once the meetings had been held and the reports written, the rest of the book was read. The children enjoyed comparing their own response to that of the cows in the book.

In this observation we have seen some quite sophisticated writing practices. Children were writing in role, collaborating with other people and writing in particular formats and styles. You might want to argue that older children should be expected to do this but it is a skill that is learned and the writing experiences that younger children are given will enable them to write in this way.

OBSERVATION: Writing in a Reception class (ages 4 and 5)

A whole reception class went on a shopping trip to buy the ingredients to make a Christmas pudding. All 35 children went on a bus to a local supermarket; they were in small groups and each group was led by an adult. Each group had their own shopping list which they had written themselves. The children were encouraged to read the words on the list and to hunt for the items needed in the shop. In the afternoon Natasha worked independently to write an account of the morning's trip in her writing journal.

> **Comment**
> This piece of writing comes from an exciting, authentic experience. The children were clearly full of what they had done and were eager to record it in their journals. They had something to write about and so could concentrate on how to convey what they wanted to say rather than scratching their heads and trying to think of something. They had a genuine purpose for writing and a personal experience to write about.

All the children have writing journals which are used to write about events in school, to recount home events and to act as a showcase for their writing. From the very beginning of their time in school, journal writing is modelled as something special that can be looked back at and can be a source of personal pride. Teachers frequently use the journals to show children how much progress they have made since their arrival in school. Journals are expected to be illustrated and the illustrations are considered as important as the writing. Most children are keen to do journal work and love to spend significant amounts of time writing and drawing.

Think about

What's in a name? What difference do you think it would make to the children as writers to be writing in a 'journal' rather than on paper or in a 'writing book'?

Comment

The explicit encouragement to the children to reflect on the progress they have made as writers serves at least two purposes. First, they are being shown how to evaluate their own work; they look critically at work done previously in relation to what they have done now and talk about specific ways in which progress has been made. Second, and maybe more importantly, in seeing the improvement in their writing their self-esteem is raised and they feel confident in themselves as writers.

To support the children's early writing, laminated key words are stuck on the wall facing the writing area. An adult usually works with the children doing journal work. Word cards are provided on the table which have key words in alphabetical order on one side of the card and letters with an illustration from the phonic programme on the other, indicating the correct letter formation. All the children are encouraged to write independently and to use strategies to enable them to do this – word cards, thinking of the first sound of the word, using the key words on the door, and so on. This means the children are always able to read what they have written.

Comment

To support independence the children are given all the resources they need to write. The strategies which the children are encouraged to use need to have been explicitly taught. The class daily play games with the key word cards and they are not a permanent display but used as part of teaching and learning activities in the classroom. Sometimes children will use word cards to create texts rather than transcribing them themselves. Why do you think the teacher would encourage them to do this?

Figure 4.1 A recount of a shopping trip written by a 5-year-old

The recount in Figure 4.1 is written by Natasha, a 5-year-old pupil who spent two terms in the nursery attached to the school and wrote this at the end of her first term in the Reception class. She is the third and youngest child in the family, with two brothers who attend the same primary school. Her teacher describes her as a bright, articulate and enthusiastic learner with a mature outlook in the classroom. She speaks English as a second language and her first language is Hebrew. Her parents speak some English but Hebrew is the main language used in the home.

When writing the recount Natasha used the word cards and the key words on the door and did so without prompting from an adult. She asked for help to write the word 'ingredients' but was able to segment it into 'ing – greed –

yens', recognising that the first sound was /i/. When 'ingredients' was added as a key word on the door, she was able to read it and put it into a sentence with the other key words that she already knew.

> **Comment**
>
> This is a lovely example of how the phonic teaching is influencing Natasha's writing. Look carefully at what Natasha is doing. She is not segmenting the word into phonemes but into syllables. Syllables are the most accessible unit of spoken language and can be described as the rhythm of language. Has Natasha identified the syllables correctly? How would you help her to do this? Clapping, stamping, tapping, jumping while saying the word are just some of the ways to help children feel the rhythm of the words and to identify the separate syllables.
>
> Why is this useful to children? It helps them to hear the phonemes in each syllable. Once a syllable has been identified, they can be helped to segment each syllable into phonemes.
>
> Can you break the word 'ingredients' into syllables and then segment it into phonemes?

When she had finished her writing, Natasha showed it to the teacher and the following conversation was held:

Teacher: Gosh Natasha, what fantastic writing! You did this independently. Wow! I am so impressed that you knew how to write so many words on your own. Look at the beautiful way you've written your letters. And you've remembered lots of finger spaces between the words. Full stops too! Can you read it to me?

> **Comment**
>
> The teacher is effusive in her praise of Natasha, but look carefully at exactly what she is saying. Not only does she praise her but she states very clearly what she is praising her for. What has Natasha done that is worthy of praise?
>
> - She worked independently.
> - She was willing to have a go and to use the resources that were made available.
> - She formed most of the letters correctly.
> - She put finger spaces between the words.
>
> Well done Natasha! Is there anything else that you might have praised Natasha for?

Natasha: We went to the shop to buy ingredients. We went in a bus. That's me on the bus, look – can you see my head in the window?

> **Comment**
>
> Natasha is here beginning to engage in conversation about the topic of the writing. How might you have responded to this if you were the teacher?
>
> By talking with Natasha about the content of the writing rather than just transcriptional aspects you would be responding as a reader rather than just as a teacher.

Teacher: I can. That bus looks full of children going to Sainsburys. Look how clever you are. Look at the beginning of your journal – beautiful drawing but no words and now, you're writing clever words on your own. I expect in your next piece of writing you'll put nice big finger spaces between each word, won't you?

Natasha: Yes. My finger spaces are a bit skinny in this one aren't they?

Teacher: They are. But you've remembered we need them. Do you think we need to do something special at the beginning of your sentence too? Can you remember what it is?

Natasha: No. Do we make the letter big? Oh, I know. Captain Capital. I need a capital 'w' for 'we'.

Teacher: Brilliant girl! You're absolutely right. I'm going to write that on a special Post-it for you. You choose which colour and I'll stick it on your journal for next time.

> **Comment**
>
> The teacher is now beginning to challenge Natasha and to give her targets for next time. The targets are ones she identifies along with Natasha and her conversation is modelling to Natasha how she might review her own work and set her own personal targets. Note how she scaffolds Natasha's evaluation of her own finger spaces and leads her towards realising how they can be improved herself. See also how she encourages Natasha to remember teaching she has had about capital letters and then relate that to her own work. Yet, it is all done within a context of praise for what has been achieved.

Natasha chose a pink heart-shaped Post-it and the teacher wrote, 'Finger spaces and capital letter at the beginning!' She then stuck the Post-it onto the side of her work and wrote a comment on the bottom, reading it aloud to Natasha as she wrote, 'It was a fun trip, wasn't it'.

Comment

In her written comment the teacher is making an affective response to the shared experience and is showing Natasha that she has read what she has written and that what is most important is the content.

How might the teacher continue this conversation?

We have all been in the position of sitting in front of a blank sheet of paper or a blank computer screen with an equally blank mind, not knowing at all what to write about. In order to help children to become writers, teachers need to understand that experience and so from it know that writers need authentic experiences to write about. When we have to scratch our heads and ponder over what to write next, continually checking the word count button, our writing is not likely to be the best. The best writing comes when we have lots to write about because we are enthusiastic and excited about the content; we may be writing about things that really matter to us or experiences we found exciting, enjoyable or even frightening. Children feel exactly the same about writing. Natasha was writing about an experience she had clearly enjoyed. She was writing about it in a special place and she knew exactly what the purpose of writing in her journal was. Providing these experiences, purposes and tools allows children to develop their compositional skills as authors.

Teachers also need a knowledge of the transcriptional conventions of written English so that they can help children to master them. Do you know what a sentence is? How would you explain it to a child in Key Stage 1 or even in Reception? Could you explain to Natasha where capital letters go? Many children put them at the beginning of each line; that's very understandable but how would you allay that misconception?

What are full stops for? It is helpful to remember that punctuation is generally for the reader rather than the writer. The writer uses punctuation to tell the reader how the text is to be read. Often the best way to explain what punctuation is needed is to read a text aloud.

Teaching writing also needs a strong phonic knowledge. Can you identify syllables in words and can you then segment each syllable into its constituent phonemes? The word 'ingredients' is a challenging one. It has four syllables:

In – gred – i – ents

These are made up of 11 phonemes:

/i//n/ /g//r//ee//d/ /ee/ /e//n//t//s/

A grapheme is the way of writing down a phoneme, so there are always the same number of graphemes in a word as there are phonemes. However, a grapheme can consist of one or more letters, so there are not always the same number of letters as graphemes and phonemes. That is where it can get confusing! 'Ingredients' is difficult because the graphemes used to represent the phonemes are not always the most common, for example, the phoneme /ee/ is represented by the letter 'i' twice. As a teacher you need to be aware of this but recognise that young children might not be ready to understand complex segmenting. Natasha segmented the word how she said it and so heard it; the most positive response would be not to correct her but to say the word to her and encourage her to repeat it slowly and clearly, making it into a game.

The shopping trip was as much a writing lesson as any shared or guided writing lesson. It served two purposes: it was an integral part of a cross-curricular project (making a Christmas cake) and gave the children a real experience to write about. The children had created a shopping list which they used when they went on the trip and the recount of the trip was for a personal record.

There were many resources within the classroom to support children's independent writing and it is important to note that these were constantly used, referred to and changed. They were not just permanent displays in the classroom. The children were aware of them and accustomed to using them.

In this observation the particular pedagogical strategy which stands out and is worthy of note is the way in which the teacher responded to Natasha's writing and used it to set targets for future development. Key points noticed in the commentary are:

- The teacher responded as a reader – she made comments on the content and expressed her own response to it in writing.
- She praised Natasha for her achievements and was very explicit about what was being praised.
- She helped Natasha to identify herself the targets for development. This meant they were attainable in the near future and were clearly understood. She involved Natasha in recording them.

The way in which this activity was set up illustrates how writing is deeply embedded in all classroom activities. The journal had already been established within the classroom as a place to record important experiences and events, and so Natasha was happy with and understood the process. Natasha also knew the resources that were available to her and used them well.

The teacher was clearly aiming to help Natasha become an independent writer and she did this in several ways:

- the resources of the classroom
- by treating her as an independent writer
- by evaluating Natasha's current understanding and achievements
- by indicating clear and specific small steps towards improvement

- by modelling to Natasha the process of evaluation of her own achievements.

Through the use of praise and by responding to Natasha's writing as a reader,
the teacher ensured that the writing experience was positive for all concerned.
Notice how positively she supported Natasha in seeing that the spaces between
words needed to be larger. How much better than a brusque comment, 'Your
word spaces are too small'. Writing is very hard work for adults and children and
any discouragement or setback will be very off-putting.

Talk for writing

Your experiences of writing school and college assignments, letters, emails or
even shopping lists will have shown you that a lot of thinking and
experimenting goes on before you commit words to paper or screen. Most of
us will rehearse ideas in our minds and try out different sentence structures.
For young children this is even more important. Talk can help them to
structure their ideas and thinking and to investigate the best words to use and
the best ways to use them. Before any writing activity children need lots of
talk – in large groups, in small groups and individually. They need to hear
teachers modelling sentence structures to them and also receive feedback
from conversational responses to their own ideas.

One of the most significant influences on classroom practice is the
consultant, Pie Corbett. He has published many practical resources to support
teachers in their planning and teaching and these can be found in many
schools. His work on story is said to be based on the work of the developmental
psycholinguist, Traute Taeschner, from Rome. Her work (Taeschner 1991)
argued that language acquisition, particularly the acquisition of a second
language, is about internalising the patterns of the language. Corbett based his
story-making project on this, transferring the learning of patterns of language
to learning patterns of narrative with accompanying actions. Corbett links the
ideas of book talk, and storytelling, with talk for writing, arguing that these
strategies give children content, purpose, motivation and skills for writing. He
says, 'It is this developmental exploration through talk, of the thinking and
creative processes involved in being a writer that we are calling *Talk for
Writing*' (2008: 3).

The point is clearly made, that learning to write is much more than just
learning to form letters, to spell and to construct grammatically meaningful
sentences. The following observation from a Year 5 class (age 9–10) shows
the close relationship between reading and writing. It is part of the same unit
of work from which we discussed a reading lesson in the previous chapter.

OBSERVATION: Year 5 class (ages 9 and 10) writing in the style of Dickens

The lesson began with the teacher recapping the two previous lessons. Part of these lessons was described in the previous chapter; a group were looking at a section from *Oliver Twist* and were exploring their understanding of it, scaffolded by the teacher's questions. The whole class had also spent time looking at a passage from *Oliver Twist*, identifying the linguistic characteristics. These were recorded in a word cloud which was referred to during this writing lesson and the children were reminded of them.

> **Comment**
> This reminds us that reading and becoming familiar with the characteristics of the text type the children will be asked to write is really important.

The teacher wrote the following sentence on the board:

Miss Cooke came into school at 8.00 this morning.

The children were asked how that sentence could be changed into the style of Dickens and the teacher demonstrated this through shared writing. The teacher wrote on the whiteboard, explaining his choice of vocabulary and structure as he wrote. The sentence became:

Miss Cooke came into school very early this morning. It was dark, cold, windy and so she was wrapped in a scarf, coat and gloves to keep warm from the chill; then the radiators came on at around 9 o'clock which made her feel warmer.

There followed some discussion about how close to the style of Dickens it was. The teacher had deliberately not made it 'too good' because he wanted the children to reflect on it critically.

> **Comment**
> We all learn from our mistakes and often if we present children with a perfect piece of work it can be off-putting. This teacher gave the children the opportunity to make suggestions for improvement of this writing and this provoked a lively discussion.

The children were then given another sentence and told to rewrite it in the style of Dickens. Some children worked in a group with the teacher in a guided writing session. These were the children who needed more input before they could work effectively independently. Other children worked independently but with the teaching assistant on hand for support if needed.

> **Comment**
> Note how the teacher differentiated the activity in relation to the amount of support given. All the children were given the same task but some children were given a lot more help. Relate this back to what you know about the concept of 'scaffolding'. In order to plan this, the teacher needed to know his class very well and to have monitored their learning during the previous lessons.

Halfway through the writing time the children put their work in process on the tables and all walked round the classroom reading each other's. Sticky notes were placed on each table and the children wrote comments and suggestions.

> **Comment**
> This was a procedure used quite frequently by this teacher. He felt that the children were not very skilled at continually reviewing their work and that it would be easier to do with somebody else's writing. The children then returned to their work to find lots of suggestions. They read and considered them and maybe changed their writing accordingly before carrying on.

This was a challenging lesson for both the children and the teacher. We can identify some points of good practice which can inform our teaching of writing:

- The writing was preceded by reading and by lots of talk about the texts which were read.
- A large amount of talk took place both about the meaning of the text and the linguistic features used.
- The children were given the opportunity to collaborate or work alone in the independent work.
- Those who needed extra support were given it.
- The children were being taught how to review and revise their own writing by commenting on the writing of their peers.

OBSERVATION: Handwriting lesson in Year 1 (ages 5 and 6)

There are times when children, especially young children, need explicit teaching in handwriting and letter formation, the transcriptional skills. It is often difficult to know how to make these lessons motivating for both teacher and children.

The class is sitting on the carpet facing the whiteboard. They are looking at the teacher who is sitting on a low chair facing them to one side of the board. She says, 'Do you remember what we said yesterday – that the next thing we start is very exciting?' There are lots of nods and 'oohs' and 'aahs' from the children. 'We're going to start joined up writing. I love doing joined up writing because it's lovely and flowing and I don't have to lift my pencil up. We're going to look at the letter 'l' and learn how we make it join up.' By this time the children are really excited and eager to begin.

Comment
Many schools begin 'joined up' handwriting from the start and if they do not completely join they teach the children to form the letters with the entrances and exits already present. For example: '$\mathcal{l}$ instead of 'l'. There are strong arguments for doing this. There is a well-established link between spelling and handwriting. The hand 'remembers' the movements for common letter strings. There are also links between compositional skills and the extent to which handwriting becomes automatic.

Read
Medwell, J., Strand, S. and Wray, D. (2009) 'The links between handwriting and composing for Year 6 children', *Cambridge Journal of Education*, 39(3): 329–44.

The teacher then wrote the word 'tell' on the whiteboard and asked the children to write it with their fingers in the air. As they wrote she talked them through the shape of the letter, 'Instead of starting at the top, start at the bottom. If you get a little loop it doesn't matter'.

Comment
Once again we see the importance of talk. As the teacher talks through the letter shape with the children she not only gives them clear guidance, but also gives them a reminder of what to do and a verbal indication of the shape. A handwriting lesson has been described as a mini physical education lesson. The teacher is talking through the movement, describing what happens at each stage. That is exactly what happens to me at the gym when I am being introduced to a new exercise. Learning to form a letter is no different.

A board with handwriting lines on is then pulled down. The lines are arranged with two dotted lines in between two bold lines. The centre of each letter goes in between the middle two lines and the top and bottom lines show the extent of the ascenders and descenders.

The teacher modelled how to write several letters on the lined board and each time she talked through the movements she was making; start at the bottom, go right up to the top, back down on top of the line and then a flick out at the bottom.

The children were then given sheets on which were printed the handwriting lines. A letter 'l' was written at the start of each line. The teacher gave them clear instructions, 'On your sheet there is one to show you. Do one – if you are unsure put your hand up and somebody will come to show you. First things – put your name – two names – and remember what goes between them – a finger space'.

The children went to their places at the tables and before they began to write they were reminded about correct posture. 'Your bottom should be on the seat, your feet should be flat on the floor and make sure you hold your pencil correctly.'

As the letter progressed, the teacher was continually talking through what was happening to the children. I am going to list the things she said here. Consider how they were supporting the children develop their skills.

What's the next letter we can see? It's a 't'. It's nearly the same as the 'l' but a little shorter and with a little line across it. Look, start from the bottom, up to the top, down, kick and across.

The next letter is 'i' and it's easier than the other two, so if you can do an 'l' and a 't', it's easy.

It's a little dot. We don't want a football.

Who thinks they're going to be able to do joined up writing? I think you all are – because if you do each letter with the join in and the join out then you can put them together.

The next letter is 'h'. I think this is a little more tricky.

Don't hold your pencil too far down or you can't see what you are doing. Make sure your fingers are on the painted bit not the wooden bit.

Does it matter if we make a mistake in our handwriting? No, it doesn't – because we're practising.

One more letter. This is our challenge today because I think it's the trickiest letter – 'b'. It is a 'b' but it looks a little bit different because it's got a joining bit. Some children try and do their 'b' like this … and it looks like a muddle, so we have to remember very carefully the order in which we do it.

By listing all the comments of the teacher I hope you will begin to appreciate that she was providing a running commentary on the handwriting process. By articulating the formation of each letter and highlighting the challenges and purposes, she is providing them with a scaffolding to support their practise.

> **Task**
>
> Look at each of the comments she is making and see in what way it might support the children's learning. What is the role of the teacher during a handwriting lesson?

OBSERVATION: Guided writing with Year 3 (ages 7 and 8)

The teacher was working with a focus group of 11 children; five of these children had English as an additional language. The group had the target to achieve a Level 2 in writing by the end of the academic year. This lesson took place in May. Level 2 is the outcome that is expected for most children at the end of Year 2 and so it could be said that these children were working below expectation.

Target-setting is a central part of life in primary schools. Teachers are required to set targets for their class and for individual children and share these with both the children and their parents. This is part of a policy belief that standards can be raised through a focus on outcomes which are identifiable, measurable and achievable. However, as Einstein once said, 'Not everything that counts can be counted and not everything that can be counted counts' and the too rigorous application of specific targets can be stultifying rather than enhancing.

> **Task**
>
> Talk with a class teacher about how s/he uses target setting in the class-room, particularly with reference to the development of writing.

Read

Wyse, D. and Torrance, H. (2009) 'The development and consequences of national curriculum assessment for primary education in England', *Educational Research*, 51(2): 213–28.

In a previous lesson the children had listened to stories with dilemmas. They had predicted what was going to happen in the stories and, after sharing their predictions, had written the end of a given story on sticky notes. The learning objective of this lesson was to write the end of a story, focusing on the characters and on making the story interesting for the reader.

The lesson began with the children sitting on the carpet recapping on what they had done in the previous lesson. The word 'dilemma' was revisited and defined as a problem in a story that needs to be fixed. The teacher then introduced the word 'fable' to the group. 'We are going to be looking at more stories with special messages. These stories are called fables. If you listen really carefully and do some really deep thinking you will know the message the story is trying to teach us.'

The teacher showed the children the book *Fables* by Arnold Lobel and read the fable entitled 'The Frogs at the Rainbow's End.' It is a story of three frogs who are sure they will find gold, diamonds and pearls at the end of the rainbow. The teacher read the story to the children up to the place where the first frog met the second frog. She put the children into groups of three and gave each one a number – 1, 2 or 3. The first two had to role-play the conversation between the two frogs, number 3 had to observe and report back to the whole group. The children responded well to this and there were some exciting ideas.

Comment

By engaging in role play as the frogs, the children knew exactly what they were each thinking and feeling. This gave them a solid basis on which to write.

Each group had been given a booklet with images from the text and spaces to write in. Some of these writing spaces were speech bubbles and others were limited text boxes. Each group decided what to write and wrote it together. One child acted as scribe but all were engaged in the act of composition. First, they wrote in a speech bubble what the first frog said. Suggestions ranged from 'Come with me!' to 'You can't be my friend'. Each group reported back, the whole group chose one response and the teacher added this to the slide on the interactive whiteboard.

> **Comment**
>
> The fact that the children had only a limited space to write in meant that they were not inhibited by a blank sheet of A4 paper or an empty page in their exercise book. Alongside the encouragement this gave them was the support of knowing that they had already tried out their ideas in the small group. They were not making themselves vulnerable by writing just their own ideas but in working with a group they were supporting each other.

The teacher then carried on reading and stopped again when the two frogs met the third frog. The activity was repeated and the children talked in pairs about how the two frogs would react to the third frog. When the group was sharing their ideas the teacher used the strategy of lolly sticks to ensure that each child had a turn to speak. Each name was written on the end of a lolly stick and the sticks were put into a pot. The teacher took one out and the child whose name was on the stick spoke.

> **Comment**
>
> This is a useful strategy if some children tend to dominate class discussion or some children never volunteer. It ensures that every child is given an opportunity to speak. Once a child has had a turn, that lolly stick is not put back in the pot. Teachers need to be very sensitive and ensure that questions are modified to suit the child chosen and differentiation will occur in the responses to the children. In this group there were some children who would call out and dominate and others who were very quiet and liked to hide in the background. This strategy meant all children had a chance. Milly, who is normally very quiet, expressed creative ideas eloquently, for example, 'The treasure would only be gold dust and so the frogs would have to leave it behind as it was too small to share.'

The teacher then read to near the end of the story when the three frogs arrive in the cave. Again, the children discussed what would happen in pairs and shared thoughts on what would happen. As groups they completed the story in their booklets. The teacher then read the whole story to the children right up to the end. The frogs went into the cave and … you will have to read the story for yourself if you want to find out the shock ending!

> **Comment**
>
> This last observation is similar to the first one in this chapter. Can you identify the similarities and differences? What key aspects of teaching writing can you see demonstrated in this lesson?

Summary

The writing process is very complex and, like the reading process, contains many elements which all need to be taught and yet need to be seen as an integrated whole. As you observe writing lessons, consider the relative place each element plays in the lesson and how a teacher demonstrates to children the integrity of the process.

We have seen in the observations in this chapter how the elements of composition and transcription work together and yet need not coexist. We have also seen that writing is much more than putting marks on a piece of paper or tapping the keys on a keyboard.

Above all, we have seen the importance of talk for writing. Children need to have experiences to write about and they need to have talked about those experiences so they can rehearse the vocabulary and the grammatical structures they will use in their writing.

It can all be summed up in the fact that writing is a process and needs time to develop and come to fruition. We want children to join with James Michener, the American author, when he said: 'I love writing. I love the swirl and swing of words as they tangle with human emotions.'

Further reading

Cremin, T. and Myhill, D. (2011) *Thinking Critically About Writing: Writers' Voices in the Classroom*. London: Routledge.

CHAPTER 5

LITERACY ACROSS THE CURRICULUM

The purpose of this chapter is to help you think about the nature of the curriculum you provide in your classroom and in your school and the role literacy plays in that. The National Curriculum changes with different governments but classrooms and schools continue to be places where teaching and learning happens. What sort of learners do we help the children to be and how do we help them to become effective literacy users for the twenty-first century?

In considering literacy across the curriculum it is important to clarify what is meant, first, by the curriculum and, secondly, by literacy. People have different ideas of what the curriculum is. The Latin root of the word (currere = to run) has the implication of a course or track; we start at the beginning and follow the prescribed route to the end. Often the word 'curriculum' is used synonymously with the word 'syllabus' and this also has connotations of something that is externally defined and can be tested.

At the time of writing the English primary curriculum is in a state of flux and it is worth spending some time considering the issues because they will impact on what is officially defined as literacy in primary classrooms.

The New Labour government initiated the Rose Independent Review of the Primary Curriculum in 2009 which was intended to inform the introduction of a new primary curriculum in September 2011. This review recommended that the curriculum be formed around six broad areas of learning in which subject teaching would be complemented by cross-curricular work. This would give an increased focus on literacy and numeracy, including a big emphasis on speaking and listening.

As plans for a new curriculum were made it was argued that this approach was supported by international evidence, because eight out of 10 countries that have recently reviewed their primary curriculum have moved to a design based on areas of learning. Ofsted (2002) in its report on the curriculum in 31 successful primary schools, found that although teachers planned and taught largely through separate subject areas, they were adept at making clear links across subjects. Alexander, in his response to Ofsted, argued that a broad curriculum is essential,

> One reason why I get impatient with those who think that the way to raise standards in the basics is by cutting back the rest of the curriculum – my main reason of course is that it sells children short – is that this essential symbiosis between the basics and the rest has been common knowledge for a quarter of a century. (2002: 4)

This was echoed by views expressed by parents in a survey carried out by the DCSF in 2009; over 80 per cent agreed that children should learn life skills such as effective communication, teamwork and creative thinking at primary school, over 90 per cent thought young children should learn through play and 92 per cent thought that integrated learning would help children develop their reading and writing skills.

The new curriculum was planned for introduction in September 2011 with an emphasis on key skills, a real-world context to learning and clear connections between and within areas of learning. The new coalition government was elected in May 2010. The planned theme-based curriculum was abandoned and a review looking to establish a 'proper knowledge-based curriculum' was set up. The Education Minister argued that,

> People know that the place of knowledge at the heart of our curriculum is not what it was and not what it should be. More and more children should be given access to that kind of education. A proper knowledge-based curriculum should be available to all rather than just a few. (Gove 2009)

The question of what counts as the curriculum, however, still remains unanswered. The National Curriculum (2000) stated in its introductory section that, 'The school curriculum comprises all learning and other experiences that each school plans for its pupils. The National Curriculum is an important element of the school curriculum'. For some schools this is an important distinction and leads to consideration of the learning experiences offered to children. The National Curriculum is a minimum requirement and is placed within a broader framework which considers what children in the twenty-first century need to know.

> **Read**
>
> The document about the curriculum at the Wyche Church of England Primary School http://www.wyche.worcs.sch.uk.
>
> Consider how the elements of the school curriculum relate to the requirements of the National Curriculum. How does this work in schools in which you have been?

The focus of this chapter is on literacy in the whole curriculum. It is usual to have daily literacy lessons in most schools but it is also clear that no other lesson can take place without the children using literacy skills. I often tell my students that literacy is the most important subject in the curriculum – and I am only half joking! Without effective literacy skills no other curriculum subject can be fully addressed. It is very important, therefore, that children are given opportunities to use literacy in ways which are powerful in all sorts of areas and subjects. In this chapter, we begin to explore some ways of doing that.

OBSERVATION: Writing in a Nursery class (ages 3 and 4)

In this classroom every morning the teacher puts up a flip chart with a message or a question on it. As the children arrive with their parents or carers they respond in writing to that message. On the day I was there the message was that shown in Figure 5.1. As each child arrived they went to the board, read it with their parents and responded in writing.

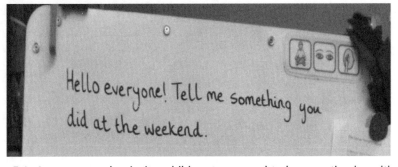

Figure 5.1 A nursery teacher invites children to respond to her question in writing

> **Comment**
> We know that children who are the most successful literacy learners are those who understand the purposes of literacy. What were these children learning by taking part in this activity?

The little girl in Figure 5.2 is clearly concentrating very hard as she writes her message. What does she need to know and be able to do in order to complete this activity?

Figure 5.2 A 4-year-old responds to the invitation

Comment

There are several positive things that can be said about this child as a writer:

- She is holding the pen correctly.
- She appears to be forming the letters correctly although we cannot be precise about that unless we are watching her actually write.
- She is writing from left to right.
- She appears to have something to say; she is writing purposefully.
- She is aware that there is a 'correct' way of writing things; she is thinking about what letter comes next.

It is difficult to make such judgements from a photograph but I observed her and was able to see her confidence and attitude. When you observe literacy activities it is important to look also at the attitude of the children participating. Ask yourself questions such as:

- Are they carrying out the activity confidently or are they doing it slowly and having to think very hard about what comes next?
- Do they appear to be enjoying the activity?

Consider what sort of behaviours you might expect to see in a child who is confident and enjoying an activity.

Read

Chris Pascal and Tony Bertram did a lot of work looking at the engagement of young children in activities (Effective Early Learning Project). They used the Leuven Involvement Scale for Young Children (Laevers 1994).

Pascal, C. and Bertram, A.D. (eds) (1997) *Effective Early Learning: Case Studies of Improvement*. London: Hodder and Stoughton.

If we look at the finished board (Figure 5.3) there are several things we can note about it as a literacy learning activity and some of these might take you by surprise.

Task

Look at this board and list all the things you think are worthy of note concerning the writing on it.

It is clear that there are lots of different styles of print on that board – upper case, printing, joined writing, children's writing and abbreviations. Notice the ampersand in the middle of the board. There was a time when teachers were very anxious about the types of print to which young children were exposed. Think, however, about all the print that children will see around them – in the home, in the local shopping centre, in places like a doctor's surgery. All print will be different and children need to learn what differences are significant and what are not. This can be challenging.

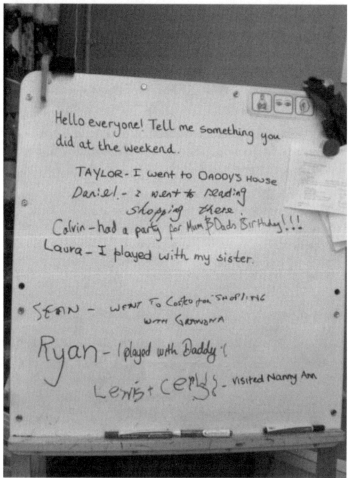

Figure 5.3 Several children in the class also responded

When I learn about objects and what they are called I soon know that objects can be different but still be called the same thing. A chair might be an upright wooden dining chair or it might be an office chair on wheels, a sagging old armchair or an ultra-modern barstool.

Letters do not always work in the same way. This is an 'a' but so is this 'a' and '*a*' and 'a' and 'a' and A. It can be very confusing. It is through experience of print in many different contexts and in many different ways that children learn to understand significant differences.

Secondly, look at the use of the exclamation mark in the third line down. Calvin 'had a birthday party for Mum and Dad's birthday!!!'

Task
What do the exclamation marks tell us as a reader? How do we read and respond to this piece of text?

Punctuation is generally there for the reader. It tells us how to read a text – the expected expression and response. It can set the tone. I later observed the teacher read through the comments on the board. She remarked on the punctuation marks by saying, 'Calvin's Mum and Dad must have had a really good time at their birthday party.'

Consider
What did that remark tell the children about the use of punctuation? What impact would their own life experiences have on their understanding?

Read
Dyson, A.H. (1993) *Social Worlds of Children Learning to Write in an Urban Primary School.* New York: Teachers College Press.

The boards in that Nursery class were just part of the literacy environment providing opportunities for children to behave as readers and writers. The next observation allows us to think about that in a little more depth.

OBSERVATION: Literacy in role play in a reception class (ages 4 and 5)

This classroom was set up to be full of literacy resources and opportunities for the children and I want to describe just three that I observed.

The role-play area was set up as a home and contained many of the tools for literacy that you might expect to see in many homes. By the armchair was a pile of newspapers and magazines; next to the phone was a telephone directory, notepad and pencil and a calendar was hanging above on the wall; next to the cooker was a pile of recipe books and by the entrance a pile of junk mail. Four-year-old Andy was sitting in the armchair, his legs crossed, reading a newspaper. He looked away from the paper, appeared to be listening, got up and answered the phone. He spoke, listened and wrote a note on the pad. He then opened the telephone directory, ran his finger down the list of names, stopped at one and then made a phone call before returning to his newspaper.

> **Talk**
>
> Find a friend and share your impressions about this observation. What was Andy showing in this short incident, of his understanding of literacy?

I expect you will have come up with quite a long list of positive comments about the value of creating a print-rich classroom environment. We can now think about this a little more and see what is missing and how it can be encouraged.

> **Read**
>
> Marsh, J. (2003) 'Connections between literacy practices at home and in the nursery', *British Education Research Journal*, 29(3): 369–82.

In this article Marsh argues that there tends to be a dissonance or mis-match between the literacy practices of school and those of home. Go back to the observation of Andy in the Reception class and think about the resources that were provided there. What was missing?

You might observe that there was no computer, no iPod, no television or game console, no mobile phone. Now consider all the uses of literacy you have engaged in over the last 24 hours and list them. When I did that, my list included the following:

- Sent several text messages.
- Read messages on a social networking site and wrote a few responses.
- Sent several emails.
- Looked for articles on a search engine.
- Checked the schedule for this book and made notes of the observations I want to include in pencil.
- Wrote several hundred words of this book on my lap-top.

That is not an exclusive list. What do you notice about the sort of literacy activities I engaged in? How similar was your list? Most of the reading and writing I have done today has been on screen. In the article above, Marsh claims that literacy behaviours of young children in the home tend to be centred around popular and cultural texts and that these behaviours do not influence the literacy opportunities offered in school.

> **Task**
>
> Plan to make a classroom for young children as print rich as possible by including the types of texts and opportunities they would encounter in the home.

In one part of the classroom was a display bench on which was a collection of several musical instruments. Alongside this was a music book showing both the words and the music of a song the children had been learning. Often the children would stand at this bench playing the instruments and singing as they 'read' the music. Jason had drawn a picture of a large colourful rainbow and below it he had drawn several musical notes ♪♫♫♪♪. The teacher asked what it was he had drawn. He looked rather perplexed at this question as though the answer was obvious and replied, 'I've written the rainbow song.'

> **Comment**
> Jason was aware of different types of symbolic representation. He wanted to write a song and knew that the symbols used for this were different from the letters he would use to record words. He had learned this because of the provision the teacher had made in the classroom. The music area had taught the children that music was written in a particular way. He had not learned this just because the resources were there. The teacher referred to it explicitly. Each week a different song was put there; the class sang it together and the teacher showed them the music and showed them that she was putting it on the music area so that they could play and sing it for themselves. She did a shared reading lesson with the words and musical notation.

On another occasion I was in the classroom observing some of the literacy behaviours of the children. I sat at tables watching the children in their play and independent activities. I had a notebook and a pencil and was continually writing, recording all that I heard and saw. I noticed that Tracey was sitting at the next table, writing in a handmade book she had found in the writing area. I went and sat next to her, asking what she was doing. She answered, 'I'm doing what you do – I'm writing down what the children are doing'.

> **Comment**
> Nobody had told Tracey what I was doing. She had watched me and worked out what I was writing. She wanted to do the same and her notebook was full of play writing which looked very like my untidy notes. What had she learned from this? She was learning one purpose of writing and was experimenting by using it for herself. This was a powerful learning experience for Tracey. She came from a home where she would not often see adults writing continuous prose and the fact that she took what I was doing and made it her own demonstrated a growing understanding of what writing could do for her.

The next observation is another example of how children represent their understandings through the use of symbols. This is older children recording their learning in Science.

OBSERVATION: Science in Year 4 (ages 8 and 9)

The class had been studying the germination and growth of seeds. They had planted seeds and watched them grow and the teacher wanted them to record this in a way which would demonstrate their understanding. They did this by creating an animation of a plant growing. Each pair of children created an animation on screen showing the growth of a plant from planting the seed to the full healthy plant. In creating these animations the children were thinking hard about how the 'reader' would understand their text. Each animation was slightly different and the children were able to discuss different approaches at various stages in the process.

Comment

The children were creating a text but it did not contain any words. What were the similarities and differences between this act of composition and how it would have been if they had recorded the growth process more traditionally by drawing and writing? Langer said, 'The distinction I wish to make is between literacy as the act of reading and writing and literacy as a way of thinking and speaking' (1986: 6). How does that distinction relate to the observations we have just been considering?

The observation above shows how literacy is more than written words. In the activity they were finding ways of expressing ideas and in doing so they needed to consider how those ideas needed to be structured and related to each other in order to best communicate the essential concepts to the reader. In choosing the best images and movements the thinking process was very similar to that of choosing the best words and linguistic structures. The following observation shows another group of children making the same sort of decisions as they authored a text.

OBSERVATION: History in Year 4 (ages 8 and 9)

The class had been studying the Vikings and had researched a lot of information about them. They had begun by sharing all the information they knew and recording it in a large mind map. They then looked at that information and, in groups, identified the questions they still had about Vikings. These questions became the focus of their research and they collected a huge amount of additional information. They then had to decide what to do with all this accumulated knowledge.

The class had used a variety of sources for information gathering and was excited at what had been found out. The children wanted to convey this excitement as they reported their research and were reluctant to 'just write it down'. They decided to create an animated interactive encyclopedia using PowerPoint.

Think

How does the chosen media affect the process of presenting information? What skills and knowledge were required by the children to do this?

They began by sorting out their information into chapters or slides. The original questions gave them a starting point for doing this but the final version did not exactly follow the themes of the questions. They eventually came up with a list of headings:

- Fast facts.
- Fast facts 2.
- Viking work.
- Vikings at sea.
- The longboat.
- Viking death.

Each group took a heading and went away to work on their slide. The slide on 'Vikings at Sea' is shown in Figure 5.4.

Each of the pictures was animated; the waves became storm like and the Viking boat was tossed as it moved through the choppy sea. Clicking on the symbols at the bottom right of the slide activated sound files: one was of the sea; the second of the farm animals and the third one of a Viking 'song'.

 # Vikings at sea

- The longboats could travel at about 10 mph.
- A ship carried everything needed at sea - drinking water, dried meat and fish to eat, tools and weapons, and furs to keep warm.
- The Vikings could sail down rivers and streams and they beached it on the side of the river they got out and slaughtered everyone.
- Cargo ships carried families and farm animals too.

Figure 5.4 One slide from an interactive encyclopedia created by a group of 8-year-old boys

The centre 'home button' took the reader back to the contents page.

A superficial look at this slide might lead you to think that this was an unchallenging writing task for these children, but look again and consider what needed to be known, to be understood and to be able to be done.

- In writing the text the children had to be aware of the limited space provided by one slide. It took a lot of discussion before they were happy with the words. The first text had to be drastically pruned and it proved challenging to convey all the information in not many words. There was a lot of oral composition and editing during the process.
- Secondly, the pictures had to be chosen. Those children who had been given the responsibility of doing this looked carefully for a picture of a Viking boat. They rejected many, drawing upon their knowledge of Viking boats. They then placed it on the sea and introduced the animation.
- Thirdly, the group doing the sound files had to think carefully about what to choose. The sounds of the sea and the farm animals were fairly simple, but choosing a sound of a Viking song was difficult. The group found the following quotation from a tenth-century Arab merchant on the Internet, 'Never before have I heard uglier songs than those of the Vikings in Slesvig (in Denmark). The growling sound coming from their throats reminds me of dogs howling, only more untamed'. They then had great fun trying to replicate and record this sound. They experimented many times before deciding on the final version.

Comment

This is a good illustration of the fact that the final product does not always give justice to the work that went into its production. This single slide involved talk of many different kinds, research and creating texts.

Once each group had produced their individual slides, the whole encyclopedia had to be put together. The children decided on the order and then created the contents 'page'. One group decided it would be good to add a slide with links to useful sources of information and so went off to research and create this. Another group made a slide with a Viking-based game on it and a third group wrote the index and the 'blurb'.

Consider

What literacy skills were used for these activities?

Read

Merchant, G. (2007) 'Writing the future in the digital age', *Literacy*, 41(3): 118–28.

Putting together a text such as this gave the children opportunities to experience the different structure of a text. The text they created was not linear and some children found it challenging to consider that there was no prescribed order and readers would create their own pathway through the text. They followed many different routes through the text because they wanted to know what it would be like for each reader. In this way, the children were coming to an understanding of how readers bring their own meanings to a text and use a text for their own purposes. For some children the experience of creating this text made them more efficient users of information books.

In the following observation we revert to presenting information through the written word. The children were, in focusing on persuasive language, also developing their skills as critical readers. This is a crucial aspect of what it means to be a good citizen, taking one's place in a democratic society. If one is aware of how authors use all aspects of a text, written or otherwise, to get across their message, one is more able to resist persuasion and manipulation. The children in the following observation were considering how vocabulary choice, design, colour and images are used on packaging. If they had been also considering television advertisements they might have included consideration of sound and camera angle.

OBSERVATION: Year 6 creating promotional texts for cookies (ages 10 and 11)

The focus of work in this class had been 'Change' and this had covered the subject areas of Science and Design and Technology. In Science they had been exploring the idea that some changes are reversible and some are irreversible and had been using cooking to do so. In Design and Technology the cookery theme continued and they designed and named a Christmas biscuit.

Comment

This is an example when different subject areas are linked by a common content. Another way of linking is by identifying common skills or concepts rather than units of knowledge. For example, the link between the Science and Design and Technology is rather tenuous in this example and may well not have been apparent to the children. The skills and concepts required in each area were not similar at all, and so one could question the link.

The learning objective of the Design and Technology lesson was to write an effective promotional description of a cookie and to be able to write concisely and revise work to constraints.

> **Comment**
> This was a literacy-focused learning objective. Although the content used was design and technology the children were, in fact, experiencing a literacy lesson.

In previous lessons the children had made and tasted biscuits from a given recipe and had designed their own decoration for a biscuit. The lesson began with the teacher showing the children pictures of different types of biscuit on the interactive whiteboard. He asked them to look at and then list words that could be used to describe the biscuits. These words were recorded on the flip chart. The teacher then showed them photographs of the packets of these biscuits, focusing on the text which described them. An example of these texts was, 'They're not just any biscuits'.

In groups, the children focused on the language used and its effectiveness. They came up with some criteria for effective promotional writing about a biscuit. It should:

- say what the biscuit looked, smelt and tasted like
- compare the biscuit to something the reader would know
- tell you what was in the biscuit.

They realised that this was a tall order as none of the texts they were analysing fulfilled all these criteria.

> **Comment**
> Note how the lesson began by reading and analysing texts of the same kind that the children were being asked to write. This is known as familiarisation with the genre and should be the starting point of all your units in literacy. Before they can write, children need to have read and discussed lots of texts. Discussions will focus on how the writer of the texts achieved the purpose of the text and will identify the linguistic features of that type of text.

The children then worked independently to create their own texts. They were allowed to choose how they wrote – some used laptops, some used whiteboards and some used paper and pencil. They were given a strict time limit for their writing and told that they had only between 50 and 60 words with which to promote their biscuit.

At the end of the 20 minutes they were given, some examples which the teacher had identified during the independent time were shown to the class on the visualiser and analysed according to the extent to which they fulfilled the criteria, in the same way as the original texts had been analysed.

Comment

What literacy skills were used in this activity? The children first analysed the linguistic features of the text type they were about to write; they discussed it and shared ideas; they composed orally with a partner and then chose how they would transcribe their work.

So far in this chapter observations have focused on how both planned lessons and the planned opportunities within the classroom environment can give opportunity for literacy learning across a variety of contexts. The remaining part of this chapter focuses on the school library.

Consider

Why do you think I have included a focus on school libraries in a chapter on literacy across the curriculum?

Figure 5.5 A school library

The school library

I had first intended to write about school libraries in Chapter 7 where the focus is on the centrality of narrative in literacy learning. I visited a school to talk with a class teacher who is also the school librarian. As I talked with her, it became more and more apparent to me that the library was central to promoting literacy within the whole curriculum. After our conversation, the teacher was kind enough to write for me her thoughts on the use of the library and I reproduce that next with my comments interspersed.

OBSERVATION: Conversation with a teacher/school librarian

I think that it is important to make the presence and reading of books common-place and evident to learners as soon as they enter school. Making the library a regularly visited space sends a message about the importance of books to the children and makes a statement about a school's values. Display boards use bright warm colours so that the library does not seem a bland or uninviting place. Three times a week some mums come into school on a rota basis to listen to children read in the library. Every year, six Year 6 pupils are chosen by me to help run the library. They are responsible for keeping the books shelved and tidy, advising pupils who need a reading book and logging books in and out of the library computer system. It is a popular role, mostly I think because they get to sit at my desk in the librarian's chair and be in charge! However, this does help to give the library a positive image – the children feel that it is theirs. Often children who are not official librarians will help out in the library simply because they enjoy it.

Comment
Notice the emphasis the teacher/librarian is putting on the physical environment of the library. Just as in the classroom, the library environment can give positive or negative messages about the value and importance accorded to literacy. The involvement of both parents and children in caring for the environment makes it a busy and used place. It is good that pupils want to be there and to be involved.

I encourage the librarians, and others, to pass on their ideas of what works in the library and what they think needs changing. There is a 'post-box' in the library in which children can write down the titles of books that they would like to read and think should be in the library. In previous years I have asked pupils to help me create library quizzes for the rest of the school to investigate and complete in conjunction with school Focus Week or World Book Day. There is a school council who can put forward what they would like to see change in school in general.

Recently the librarians and other Year 6 children took it upon themselves to give the library a bit of a 'face-lift'. Unknown to me, they closed the library to others and during break times that day they tidied books away, straightened and reorganised shelves and found posters to put on display boards. I think that children of all ages find 'playing at being in charge' and making their own mark thrilling, and making the library a desirable place, is certainly an important part of promoting reading. The pupils sent me an email together and couldn't wait for me to come and see what they had done. Others were aware that something was going on and liked the idea of taking something into their own hands – it created quite a buzz and drew people in.

Figure 5.6 The school library designed by pupils

Comment

Pupil voice is an important element in the development and working of this library. These children were seeing the library as their own and felt comfortable and empowered to take control and improve the environment. If you were the teacher, what would you do if the children had rearranged the library in a way you did not like? Would that matter? Try and ask some children about books in their school. Is there a library? What do they think about it? How would they change it if they were in charge?

In general, if I were not also a full-time teacher, I would like to 'interfere' and interact more with all the teachers at school in order to maximise use of the library's resources and make room for a greater proportion of routine independent learning. I would also like to organise more events within school in conjunction with the library using books (popular tales, themes, authors, creative writing, experiencing an event to inspire creative writing) as the inspiration and starting-point. Ideally, the librarian should be able to monitor the reading habits of children through the library computer system and liaise with class teachers to keep them informed and so that the teacher can advise the librarian of any books that she or he thinks the child should be reading or vice versa. This better ensures that learners are reading books that (a) are of a genre likely to be enjoyed, (b) contain enough familiar vocabulary and a complexity of language that is manageable and will boost confidence and enjoyment; allowing the story and its meaning to flow in a complete narrative and (c) contain enough unseen vocabulary and some more complex language in order to challenge the reader and ensure that the reading process is also a literacy teaching tool; a learning experience.

Comment

Do you think librarians should 'interfere'? There is a significant amount of evidence which suggests that school librarians have an impact on pupils' academic achievement. Barrett says that librarians need to: be highly qualified professionals, learning specialists, work collaboratively with teachers, be information mediators, teach the skills of information literacy within the context of the curriculum, be reading experts, inspire, encourage, create, and model high-quality learning experiences and be leaders in schools, regarded on a par with teaching colleagues. That is a tall order for anybody! Barrett argues strongly that librarians need to know about teaching and learning as well as about books if they are to be truly effective in a school.

Read

Barrett, L. (2010) 'Effective school libraries: evidence of impact on student achievement', *The School Librarian*, 58(3): 136–9.

So many classrooms have their own collection of books that it can render the library rather redundant, which I think can be a common problem. I have pondered over a solution, but I think it is a must to have books in the classroom and so don't exactly want to discourage this! Having members of Year 6 helping in the daily running of the library is a necessary arrangement, however, I cannot be on hand if there is a technical fault with the scanner or system, or someone has a question that they cannot answer. Ideally, a full-time librarian is needed to get the most out of the library and out of the opportunities for the children to learn therein. I would like to see whole classes using the library for research, but this does become difficult when teachers see how much they have to cover on the curriculum and are reluctant to give up time within that to visit the library; it is much quicker to tell the children about something than to facilitate them discovering (or not) it for themselves.

Encouraging teachers to make more routine use of the library with their classes could also go some way to balancing the use of Internet search engines in order to find information and learn. Though there is a wealth of fantastic information from many different, diverse voices on the Internet, when similar key words are used for a topic in a search engine, it is probable that the same few websites, including Wikipedia, will be visited and therefore the same, not always entirely accurate, information is taken on board. Books still contain more reliable sources of information and, in a well stocked library, many different standpoints and variations. The ability to use a library gives independence to the user, whereas Internet search engines in some way dictate which sources are accessed and used. It would be a shame if children were not taught the skills, and benefits, of taking the time to use a library at school.

I would like to see official library book-changing times for each year group so that regular contact with the library is timetabled rather than left to personal choice. Many children get books from home, which is no bad thing, but it would be better to be able to keep track through the library computer system, of what each child is reading and for me to then have the time to liaise with teachers in order to keep them abreast of this so that both I and they could make sure that readers were reading books with enough familiar material to keep their confidence boosted and the story line flowing, but enough new vocabulary and higher-order language that they are also being challenged and are learning from the reading experience.

Comment

The teacher/librarian is here exploring the nature of knowledge and arguing that the library can help children to be more critical readers and evaluators of sources of knowledge. Critical literacy is an important concept and is part of the empowering and liberating effect of becoming literate. A critical reader will be able to read a text and see how the author has used particular effects and linguistic structures to locate the reader in a certain way and to manipulate the understanding of the text. A critical reader will also notice how the author's choice of language can either include or exclude. She argues that access to books can help children to see different ways of knowing and so become more critical and independent. Do you agree?

Read

Vasquez, V. (2010) 'Critical literacy isn't just for books anymore', *The Reading Teacher*, 63(7): 614–16.

Schools are essentially places of learning – both knowledge and skills. I think that how a school's library is maintained and promoted can send a statement to the pupils about what the school values and says something of its ethos. A library that is central to a school, an inviting, interesting hub that is overtly valued by teachers through lip-service and involvement, sends an essential, positive message of constructive, proactive learning values connected to books, to learners from backgrounds where reading and/or learning are not on the scene/part of the scenery/on the radar/part of life. Learning to access the non-fiction section of a library is important if you believe that teaching children how to teach themselves is an important aspect of school experience. Indeed, for those aspiring to higher education, the ability to read texts in the form of books and articles is still central; as the sometimes vast libraries of such institutions testify. In terms of fiction, a library has the responsibility to not only house the necessary variety of books to accommodate, challenge and interest readers in order to build on their comprehension, but to cater for and attract those who are more reluctant (as well as maintaining the confidence and interest of those who can already decode, comprehend and hopefully enjoy reading). Certainly, having the correct reading material and incentive to read is still vital in the sense that growing children and young adults are forever learning to decode unseen vocabulary and need the opportunity to expand and progress by having a variety of books that will challenge and engage them at the right level and that will enthuse them to continue their efforts. Also, being able to decode texts accurately doesn't of course mean that the individual words or text as whole are understood; continued reading and discussion of what has been read continues to build on comprehension of language and use of this language in communication, and essential life skills.

There is interesting discussion surrounding the impact of our continually advancing information technology on what a library – school or otherwise – should be/provide for its users. The word 'library' derives from a Latin word meaning 'book' and I think it is fair to say that libraries are still thought of as being places where, predominantly, collections of books are kept. When the word 'library' was first widely used, books (in the form of parchments, record, scrolls, and so on) could be said to be synonymous with 'information' – other than the spoken word, few other means of sharing information existed – and so the word library was a suitable one for a place where information could be gained. In this postmodern era, however, we are all accustomed to the fact that the Internet and other computer technologies have become perhaps the primary means of sharing information. Thus the word 'information' is now not only synonymous with 'book' but also with the various information technologies that we have. Should school libraries seek to uphold their identities as places where books are collected and promoted against the rising tide of technology, or should they further and/or fully re-adjust their identity so that all sources of information provision become synonymous with the word 'library'?

In my mind, in order to distinguish it from an ICT [information and communication technology] suite and remain in part true to its name, a library should certainly remain a place where books are promoted as a valuable and desirable means of discovering information, or furthering/enjoying understanding of the written word. However, it is essential to reflect on the fact that children born particularly within the last decade have no recollection of a world without computer technology and the prevalence of the Internet as a means of understanding the world and communicating. To not include any elements of this in school libraries runs the risk of condemning libraries as increasingly antiquarian places that bear no relevance to their experience of the systems in which they exist. In part, I think, the children need the experience of researching in books and the pleasure of holding a book in your hands, but the Internet utilised well opens up a superb wealth and variety of information and learning opportunities. This constructive use of computer technology needs to be incorporated into the library experience and used in conjunction with and to enhance books (and perhaps vice versa).

Comment

Reflect on your own viewpoint. She has argued eloquently about the important role libraries play in schools in supporting children's literacy development. This is so much more than learning to decode or even to understand the words within a text. To become literate means a very different thing for children who are in primary schools in the twenty-first century than it was for me when I was in primary school in the mid twentieth century. How do our pedagogical practices reflect that difference?

Read

Mullen, R. and Wedwick, L. (2008) 'Avoiding the digital abyss: getting started in the classroom with YouTube, digital stories and blogs', *The Clearing House*, 82(2): 66–9.

Cross-curricular learning

As you talk with teachers you will hear the terms cross-curricular, creativity, theme-based, creative curriculum and many other variations on a theme used. Do they mean the same thing? The observations in this chapter have been very varied. In the early years settings we have seen how teachers provide resources and allowed the children to respond and make use of them as they wanted to. Is that creative? In the observations from Key Stage 2 we saw teachers focusing on literacy skills but using content from other subjects of the curriculum to do so. Is that cross-curricular teaching?

As you consider these questions you might also want to reflect on the term 'creative learning'. Is that what we want children to encounter? Is that what will serve children well in the twenty-first century and enable them to become educated and informed citizens? We know that uses of technology and knowledge in Science are growing faster than we can imagine. Joubert (2001) claims that 75 per cent of the scientific knowledge we will need in the middle of this century has not been invented yet. Jeffrey (2006) proposes that creative learning includes elements of creativity like experimentation, innovation and invention and the element of intellectual enquiry underpins the learning.

If we consider the observation of Jason writing his song using musical notation, we can see if it works. He was certainly experimenting in using musical notation to represent a song, he was being innovative as nobody else had, as far as we know, done the same thing. He was not actually inventing but he was using a symbolic system, which was new to him, for his own particular purpose. He was certainly engaged in intellectual challenge as he was working out how to represent his song. Do you think we can argue that this observation is an example of creative learning? How does that relate to Jason's developing literacy skills?

Literacy is more than reading and writing and it is not constrained to the written word. I once saw a cartoon in which a child was unwrapping a Christmas gift of a book. His parent looked on sympathetically and comforted him with the words, 'Don't worry we can swap it for the DVD!' The joke relies on the assumption that it is 'easier' to read a film than it is a book. I would question that assumption and argue that 'reading' a film can be challenging. For me, watching the film *Inception* (Warner Bros. Pictures 2010) was as challenging as reading *Ulysses* (James Joyce 1922) and I still do not fully understand either of them! Booth argues that the literacy of school is falling behind the literacy of society and the home:

> children are dealing with a greater network of meanings and our literacy curriculum needs to match that to set them up for the future ... there is a pronounced difference between the literacies children are developing at home and the literacy of school. It is a divide that needs to be understood and explored. (2006: 59)

As you consider the observations of this chapter in the light of that comment, consider also the literacy that you see in classrooms but also in the world around you. Talk with your friends, with children and with teenagers about their experiences of literacy and consider how the curriculum in school reflects this.

Summary

In this chapter we have begun to explore the edges of some big ideas. As the curriculum develops and changes, these ideas will need to become more formulated and yet remain plastic enough to accommodate the rapidly changing world of communication and knowledge. There is much to think about and it is probably best to summarise this chapter with a list of questions:

- Is literacy more than reading and writing?
- What are literacy skills?
- What does it mean to be fully literate?
- What is critical literacy?
- How can the classroom environment help or hinder literacy learning?
- Is there a place for the book and the library in twenty-first century schools?

Further reading

Barnes, J. (2011) *Cross-curricular Learning 3–14.* 2nd edn. London: Sage.

Craft, A. (1999) *Creativity across the Primary Curriculum: Framing and Developing Practice.* London: Routledge.

Goodwin, P. (ed.) (2005) *Literacy Through Creativity.* London: David Fulton.

CHAPTER 6

PLANNING AND ASSESSMENT

In this chapter we look at the way in which teachers decide what they are going to do in their classrooms. The children's learning lies at the heart of this decision-making; teachers are continually monitoring learning and adapting and changing their plans accordingly. This chapter looks at detailed lesson plans by beginner teachers and more open unit plans by more experienced teachers.

The link between planning and assessment

Planning can be described as the process of thinking and developing ideas, putting those ideas into an order and creating plans which act as a guide for a lesson. It is certainly true that planning is an important part of being an effective teacher and yet it is possible to become too focused on ideas and things to do within a lesson and forget that the whole purpose is to ensure that the children learn. Children's learning is the key responsibility of teachers and all that you do must be clearly planned with that in mind.

So the first question to ask yourself is, 'What do I want the children to learn?' Once you, as the teacher, have decided that, everything else will begin to fall into place because you can then begin to think about the different sorts of activities and experiences that will help children to learn. It is also important to tell the children what the purpose of the lesson is and what they are supposed to learn from it. Knowing this will give children something to work for and a basis on which to judge their own learning and achievement.

It is not the intention of this chapter to describe how to set about planning for learning but rather to look at some plans and see how they have been used in the classroom. Most trainee teachers are required to create detailed lesson plans for everything they teach and the first plan we are going to look at is one of those plans.

OBSERVATION: Year 3 lesson plan on connectives (ages 7 and 8)

There are times, especially at the beginning of a teaching career, when it is important to plan in detail. Figure 6.1 is an extract from a very detailed lesson plan. This is the plan for just 15 minutes of a lesson lasting an hour and a quarter.

There are several good points which can be made about this plan:

- There is clear differentiation between the ability groups.
- The teaching assistant knows exactly what she has to do during this part of the lesson.
- Teaching points (TP) are made explicit so that the teacher knows the purpose of an activity or discussion.
- Management and organisational points are included.

However, if I were this trainee's tutor I would want to make several points to the student, particularly in relation to the detail in which things are planned.

Task
Look carefully at the plan opposite and consider if the trainee understands what is meant by 'engagement' and 'ownership' of learning. What evidence from the plan can you use to support your opinion?

It is not sustainable to continue planning in such detail for your whole teaching career; often it can take longer to plan a lesson than the lesson itself actually takes! However, the reason why it is important to do this in the initial stages is to ensure that you have planned for progression, for individual needs and for organisation and management. It is easy when sitting at home in the evening to think that it looks very straightforward. However, every teacher has been in the situation of having 30-plus faces looking at you on the carpet and

Development/ Main Activity **WALT: explore different connectives to extend sentences.** **WILF: connectives written on Post-it notes.** **ASSESSMENT: Do pupils know the difference between a time and joining connective?** Introduce the nursery rhyme 'Incy Wincy Spider' and read it aloud to the children. Encourage them to stand up on their feet and join in. Q: What is the purpose of a connective? TP: A connective links clauses or sentences together. Q: What connective is used in the nursery rhyme? TP: Explain that pupils often overuse 'and' in their own writing. Q: Can you think of a more exciting connective than 'and'? Q: How else could you link the ideas together? TALK PARTNERS: give time to discuss connectives on the spider's legs. USE LOLLIPOP STICKS (fair selection). Explain that children are going to work in small groups to improve sentences from the nursery rhyme by experimenting and changing the connective. Split pupils into mixed ability groups to provide peer support. Provide LAPs with connective cards so they can contribute ideas and access the learning task. Set the time expectations for the learning task. Ask pupils to write down their best connective on a Post-it note and add to the working wall.	**Building on prior learning** The questions will enable pupils to draw on what they understand about connectives and suggest examples. **Ensuring engagement in learning** To ensure engagement I will give them ownership by choosing what sentence they will improve and experimenting with connectives. **Learning task** Pupils work in small mixed ability groups. They select a sentence from the nursery rhyme. They discuss alternative connectives to improve the sentence. They have to read the sentence aloud to ensure it makes sense. They may have to add pronouns, e.g. 'it' to make sense. Then later in the lesson pupils will go on to write their own sentences about the spider using their own connective to add another clause/information. **Differentiation** **HAPs:** Write own sentences about the spider independently. **WILF: use time and joining connective.** **MAPs:** Write own sentences about the spider in pairs. **WILF: use joining connectives.** **LAPs:** Work as a group to cut and stick connectives into sentences. **WILF: connectives make sense.**	**Mrs A to work with child LG and his group. Support child LG's contribution to the learning task and ensure positive behaviour for learning is reinforced.** **Mrs A to pass child LG the connective cards and support his contribution to the group learning task.** **Then Mrs A to work with Yellow table during writing activity to help pupils cut and stick connectives into sentences.**

Figure 6.1 Lesson plan for a literacy lesson written by a trainee teacher in the early stages of her training programme

a completely blank mind! The lesson plan provides no help at all because all it says for this time is, 'Discuss'. It is for times like this, especially when there are no reserves of experience to draw on, that detailed planning is essential.

The plan above certainly gives a lot of detail and it is true that I would be able to walk into the classroom and teach this lesson with no problem. However, the emphasis within this plan is on the teaching; it is all about what the teacher is going to do and tell the pupils to do. What do you think the pupils would learn from this lesson? How would you know what they have learned? Sometimes, a highly structured lesson gives pupils no opportunity to demonstrate their learning because all they have to do is carry out instructions.

In the early stages planning a lesson should enable you to see the lesson in your mind's eye so that you know exactly what is going to happen when. Transitions are times when things can go wrong; if the children's drawers are all in the same place you do not want to send the whole class to get their books at the same time!

A useful strategy once you have planned a lesson is to go through it as if you were a pupil in the class. Often teachers can plan all sorts of exciting things and the lesson is active and multi-sensory but only for the teacher; the children are sitting on the carpet watching the all-singing and dancing routine. Review your plans to ensure that the children are physically, emotionally and cognitively involved.

Most teachers tend to work from their unit or weekly plans and only write detailed lesson plans when they are being observed. These plans tend to be much less detailed but can be so because the information about organisation and management is embedded in practice.

OBSERVATION: Year 6 plans for a week on persuasive writing (ages 10 and 11)

The plans that follow are a week's plans for a Year 6 class on persuasive writing. They are written by a trainee teacher at the end of his final placement.

What do you think the teacher wanted the children to learn from this first lesson (Figure 6.2)? He began by showing them a map of an imaginary town which was very like the one in which they live (Figure 6.3). He asked them to look at what was there and to think what was missing, asking themselves if there was something for everybody to do. The children here were reading the map, sharing ideas, comparing the map to their own town and empathising with the needs of other types of people. The lists were written on sheets of sugar paper which were pegged up on a line going across the front of the classroom.

Comment

The use of rough notes on sugar paper, quickly pegged up, demonstrated to the children that these were working notes which could be changed and modified. They were not the final product.

LITERACY SHORT TERM PLANNING   15/11/09

	Objective	Starter	Main Lesson Activity/Key Questions	Plenary
Mon	To generate ideas for writing To consider what would appeal to the audience for a persuasive letter	What do you need to be careful of when we are writing a persuasive letter? Can you create an ambitious and interesting sentence using one or more of these verbs? (Talking time)	Give the children map/specification of town. Discuss what you notice there is for different people to do. How is it like ▇▇▇? How is it missing from this town? *Small/Friendly* *they have x,y etc* Children use the space on the maps to identify things that are missing from Middleton — *HUGE list - write up on the board/on the* Link - citizenship. Children are developers. Council is going to give planning permission for 1 thing in Middleton. In their groups brainstorm what is good about the town from the developers point of view and what they would like to add to town. Get as many ideas as possible. *Split into table groups* Collect ideas on board/sugar paper. What community groups might there be in Middleton? (elderly, disabled, teens, parents with young chn, single people who commute to work). Chn to return to development group and decide on which one development that they think would benefit everybody. Thinking hats.	3 sentences to persuade the rest of the class that your idea is the best —everybody votes for which group is most persuasive. *— well worth* *1) Older sweet* *2) Retail shop* *3) Health Ca* *4) Theme Park* *5) Go-Kart*

Good reasons for (+ or counters for (—) re feelings about developm

Figure 6.2 Day 1 of a literacy unit of work annotated by the teacher afterwards

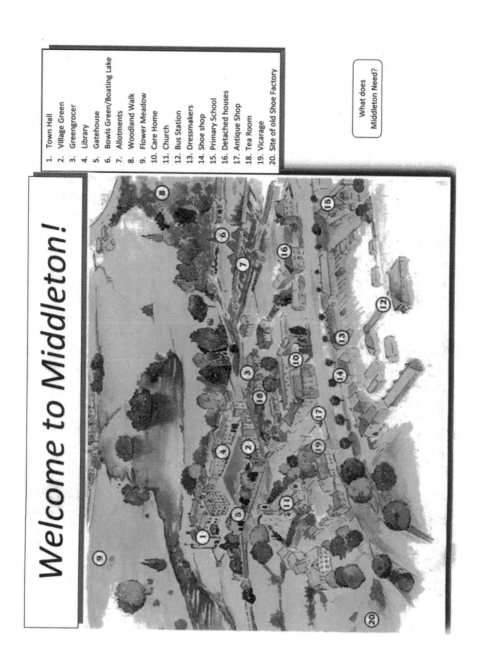

Welcome to Middleton!

1. Town Hall
2. Village Green
3. Greengrocer
4. Library
5. Gatehouse
6. Bowls Green/Boating Lake
7. Allotments
8. Woodland Walk
9. Flower Meadow
10. Care Home
11. Church
12. Bus Station
13. Dressmakers
14. Shoe shop
15. Primary School
16. Detached houses
17. Antique Shop
18. Tea Room
19. Vicarage
20. Site of old Shoe Factory

What does Middleton Need?

Figure 6.3 Resource used in the literacy unit on persuasive writing

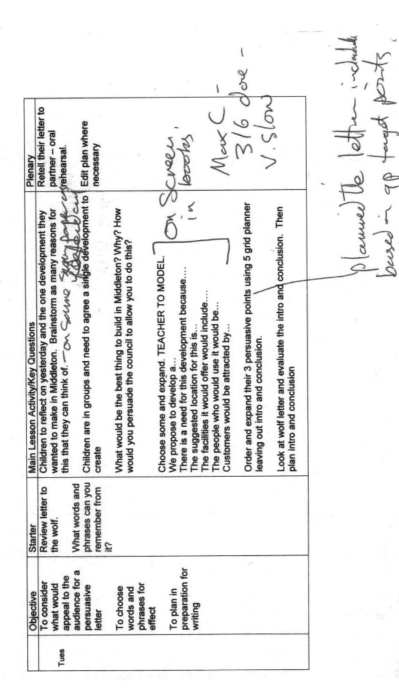

LITERACY SHORT TERM PLANNING   15/11/09

	Objective	Starter	Main Lesson Activity/Key Questions	Plenary
Tues	To consider what would appeal to the audience for a persuasive letter	Review letter to the wolf. What words and phrases can you remember from it?	Children to reflect on yesterday and the one development they wanted to make in Middleton. Brainstorm as many reasons for this that they can think of. — on same flipchart sheet Children are in groups and need to agree a single development to create	Retell their letter to partner – oral rehearsal. Edit plan where necessary
	To choose words and phrases for effect		What would be the best thing to build in Middleton? Why? How would you persuade the council to allow you to do this?	
	To plan in preparation for writing		Choose some and expand. TEACHER TO MODEL. We propose to develop a.... There is a need for this development because.... The suggested location for this is.... The facilities it would offer would include.... The people who would use it would be.... Customers would be attracted by....] On Screen, in lessons Order and expand their 3 persuasive points using 5 grid planner leaving out intro and conclusion. Look at wolf letter and evaluate the intro and conclusion. Then plan intro and conclusion	Max C – 316 Joe – V. Slow

Handwritten note: planned the letter – include based on 90 target points

Figure 6.4 Day 2 of the unit plans

LITERACY SHORT TERM PLANNING   15/11/09

	Objective	Starter	Main Lesson Activity/Key Questions	Plenary
Wed	To consider what would appeal to the audience for a persuasive letter (level To choose words and phrases for effect To experiment with the order of sections and paragraphs to achieve different effects	Have 9 features of persuasive text and have cards with persuasive phrases on. Match persuasive phrase to feature.	Teacher to model part of letter that proved difficult for children last week – the point being made in the first sentence of a paragraph and using the rest of the paragraph to support this one point (AFL – Chn muddling several ideas in one paragraph) Pair writing - Chn to write their intro and 2 paragraphs.	Edit with polishing pen

Handwritten annotations:

Lottie + Claudia 3 + trouble concentrating low confidence in group.

Great Concentration - really good work from: Jamie S Oliver

Stretched to include complex sentences / similes.

Figure 6.5 Day 3 of the unit plans

After the lesson the teacher annotated the plans. His annotations reflected on the ideas the pupils had had during group work and his comments on how they had worked as a group. He noted that they gave lots of positive reasons for the development but struggled more to give reasons against the proposed development.

The plans for Tuesday (Figure 6.4) were annotated and adapted to reflect how Monday's lesson went. The notes on the sugar paper were added to and particular children were selected to have more structured help.

Comment

This illustrates the close relationship there is between planning and assessment. Teachers are continually monitoring learning and adapting plans accordingly. It is important to remember that every lesson must take the children's learning forward in some way and this depends on knowing exactly where they are in their knowledge, understanding or skill. The teacher knew what he wanted to achieve by the end of this week and adapted the daily plans to ensure that this was achieved. On Tuesday he wanted to develop the children's ability to identify key points which could be used to persuade the council.

The annotations on Tuesday's plans indicated that Max was working very slowly and that most of the children, while justifying their proposed development well, did not introduce or conclude the persuasive letter well. Wednesday's plan (Figure 6.5) was adapted to address these needs.

Look how the teacher supported the children in the aspect of the work with which they were struggling:

- He gave them a starter activity which focused specifically on the type of language they needed to use in their writing.
- He modelled the writing for them.
- He gave them a very specific writing task.
- He asked them to write in pairs.

Comment

Shared writing is when the teacher writes and is demonstrating to the class the writing process. There are three main kinds of shared writing:

Demonstration – the teacher writes and while writing talks aloud about the choices and decisions that are being made. This is an important teaching strategy as much of the writing process goes on in the head and so is invisible to the observer.

Teacher acts as scribe – the children compose a text while the teacher writes it down. This gives the teacher the opportunity to encourage the children to

(Continues)

(Continued)

compose orally before transcribing (oral rehearsal) and also to show how editing and revision are central to the writing process.

Children write independently or in pairs, usually on whiteboards, and discuss their choice of words and their appropriateness to the writing task.

Wednesday's plan was adapted in a way which gave scaffolding of the particular aspect of the task that was causing difficulties on Tuesday. The learning objective which required the children to be able to choose words and phrases for effect was not achieved as the children had been unable to judge the effect. The starter activity helped them to do this and the modeling showed how the teacher considered this. The fact that the independent writing was now to be done in pairs meant that the children were put in a situation where they had to talk about the effect of the word choices they were making.

After Wednesday's lesson the teacher noted that one pair of children was working well and needed to be challenged more the following day. He also noticed, however, that there were two pairs of children who were lacking in confidence and had not really been talking to each other about the word choices.

Thursday's lesson plan (Figure 6.6) began with the whole class looking at the writing from the pair of children who needed more challenge. It was put up onto the whiteboard using a visualiser and the class gave it two stars and a wish. They found two positive things to say about it and one thing which could be improved.

Comment

The teacher chose a piece of work from a confident and high-ability pair. This was a useful model to the other children and helped them to see what could be done. In evaluating the writing the teacher was modelling to the rest of the class how they could improve their own writing. However, in also identifying one area of development in this writing the exercise also acted as a challenge to the more able children. They were encouraged to use more complex sentences and also to include some similes in their writing. These improvements were not just suggested by the teacher; less able children were able to orally compose and make suggestions when working together as a group that they were not able to do independently.

The independent task was to write the final paragraph and conclusion. The children who had struggled on Wednesday were given a writing frame on Thursday to support their writing. The teacher had put the writing they had already done into the frame and talked it through with them at the start of the independent writing time so they had a much more tightly 'framed' piece of work to do.

The starter activity for Friday (Figure 6.7) focused on the main learning objective for the whole week – to consider what would appeal to the audience

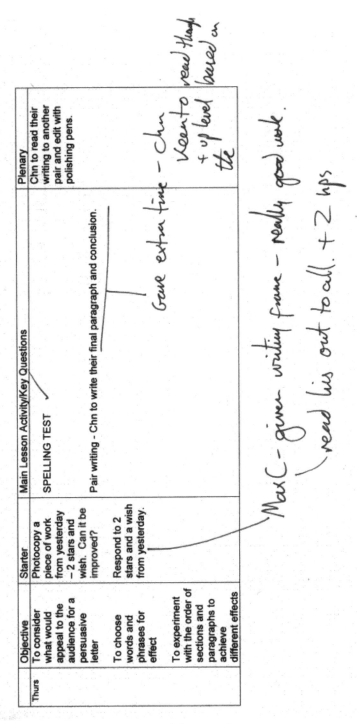

LITERACY SHORT TERM PLANNING   15/11/09

	Objective	Starter	Main Lesson Activity/Key Questions	Plenary
Thurs	To consider what would appeal to the audience for a persuasive letter	Photocopy a piece of work from yesterday – 2 stars and a wish. Can it be improved?	SPELLING TEST ✓	Chn to read their writing to another pair and edit with polishing pens.
	To choose words and phrases for effect	Respond to 2 stars and a wish from yesterday.	Pair writing - Chn to write their final paragraph and conclusion.	
	To experiment with the order of sections and paragraphs to achieve different effects			

Gave extra time – chn keen to read their writing + up level (based on tte)

Max C – given writing frame – really good work
(read his out to all. + 2 hps)

Figure 6.6 Day 4 of the unit plans

LITERACY SHORT TERM PLANNING   15/11/09

	Objective	Starter	Main Lesson Activity/Key Questions	Plenary
Fri	To consider what would appeal to the audience for a persuasive letter To evaluate a piece of persuasive writing.	Chn to choose the best persuasive letter for their development. Get together with the people in their groups to decide which are the best two letters, and who is going to read the letters to the class debate (doesn't have to be the same person that wrote the letter)	Debate: Real town hall meeting style – class set into debate layout – children sitting on opposite sides of the room or in another area – even outside? Representatives from each group to speak and be seconded by another. NC/JN to act as moderator/ facilitator Time for each student to contribute to the discussion – what's good about them? Take a vote as to the most persuasive argument – which is the winner?	Which of our letters was picked as the best? Why do you think the other class picked it?

Handwritten annotations:

1 min per st'gp + 3 min questions

good criticising of the speaker

Very good questioning from children (Goldsmiths)

More time to prepare speeches – Hadn't managed to do before.

Figure 6.7 Day 5 of the unit plans

for a persuasive letter. In evaluating the letters within larger groups the children were applying all they had learned during the week. Note, however, that this evaluation was done with a genuine purpose in mind. The letters were going to be read out at a 'town hall meeting' and the one which was the most persuasive would be the winner.

> ### Comment
> Authentic writing tasks are usually the most successful. Persuasive writing can only really be judged by the extent to which it persuades the reader of the arguments and this is what was being put to the test in this class. How much more effective was this than the teacher taking away books to mark them against a list of words and linguistic structures which should be included.

The class held a debate with each group making the case for their preferred development. After the letter had been read out, questions were asked. Children were also asked to comment on how persuasive they had found the letter and what features of the letter they found most persuasive. The debate finished with a vote. The lesson ended with an analysis of the successful letter. Displaying it on the whiteboard using the visualiser, the class highlighted those elements of the writing which they had found the most persuasive.

> ### Comment
> To what extent do you think this series of lessons succeeded in helping the children to be able to write persuasively and also to be able to recognise persuasive writing as readers? What elements of the lessons helped to achieve this?

In reviewing this series of lesson plans there are some key points that can be learned about the planning process:

- The focus of the plans was the children's learning. Once this is identified then all the activities can be geared towards addressing this.
- Monitoring of learning is an ongoing process and is an integral part of teaching.
- Flexibility is essential so that the children's responses and needs are addressed.
- If they are given clear criteria and authentic experiences children are able to evaluate their own learning.
- Effective personalisation of learning can only take place when learning is monitored.

It is often easier to plan a series of lessons than one-off lessons because of the need to be responsive to the children's needs. If children have not understood, known or been able to do what you wanted them to do on the first day there is absolutely no point at all in continuing to do what you had planned for the second day. You need to adapt your plans to revisit the learning objective using a context or activities that engage the children more effectively. If children do not learn what it was intended they should learn, an effective teacher will first review and adapt his or her teaching.

I hope that looking at this series of lesson plans has shown how assessment and planning are inextricably linked. This is what is meant when we talk about assessment for learning. It occurs when teachers monitor and respond to children's learning during lessons. This happens through formative assessment, which can take many forms.

Read

Black, P. and Wiliam, D. (1998) 'Inside the black box: raising standards through classroom assessment', *Phi Delta Kappan*, 80(2): 139–48.

Black, P., McCormick, R., James, M. and Pedder, D. (2006) 'Learning how to learn and assessment for learning: a theoretical inquiry', *Research Papers in Education*, 21(2): 119–32.

Continuous monitoring of learning is a key element of the teacher's role and effective learning cannot take place without it. Responding to the children's needs and adapting teaching accordingly is what good teaching is about. This is perhaps the most important element of effective teaching – decide what you want the children to learn, make sure you are clear how you will know if they have learned it and continually observe them and what they do and say to monitor their learning. In the light of this monitoring, adapt and change your teaching and the learning opportunities you provide to ensure learning. Remember that when you are planning, you are planning for learning – decide what that learning is and then use whatever content is most appropriate and relevant to the class to teach.

However, teachers and schools are accountable to parents, headteachers and the government, and need to ensure that children are making progress according to specified criteria. These critieria define what progression looks like and can sometimes make a very complex idea appear too simple. To illustrate this, let us consider what, in my opinion, is one of the most difficult things to teach – writing.

How do I know if a piece of writing is effective? I know that my writing is effective if it fulfils its purpose and is appropriate for the audience. I know that by the response I get to my writing. If I am reading a novel, that writing is effective if I enjoy the book and want to carry on reading – if I sympathise with the characters, can imagine the setting or feel scared, amused or charmed. Good writing serves its purpose well. There are times when good writing is very simple, as illustrated by the opening of Jill Murphy's *Peace at Last.*

The hour was late.
Mr Bear was tired.
Mrs Bear was tired.
Baby Bear was tired.

Here the writing consists of four simple sentences. The same pattern is repeated and there are no 'wow' words. Yet, it is an extremely effective piece of writing. As the opening of a story it sets the scene well. It establishes the unity of the Bear family and their shared feeling of tiredness. This emphasises the isolation of Mr Bear later when he is the only one who cannot get to sleep. Sometimes simple writing is very powerful.

However, if this writing were to achieve a Level 3 according to the writing assessment guidelines published by the Primary National Strategy (http://www.cfbt.com/lincs/pdf/writingL3toL4.pdf) some changes would need to be made. Level 3 writing shows 'some attempt to elaborate on basic information or events' and has 'some links between sentences'. The author might need to have written something like,

The hand on the clock pointed to ten and so showed that the hour was late.
Mr Bear felt very tired and Mrs Bear also experienced great tiredness. In
addition, Baby Bear suffered weariness.

Which piece of writing do you think is the most powerful?

Of course, it is important to measure children's achievements at specific points in time to ensure that their achievements have reached the nationally required standards and this is the role of summative assessment.

RAISEonline is a data analysis system which enables individual schools to analyse their performance data against national standards. This allows schools to compare the achievements of their pupils against those in other schools and so plan in order to raise achievements. This data is used by a variety of people to make judgements about the school.

Task

Ask a school to show you their RAISEonline profile and to talk it through with you. Talk with teachers about how this impacts on their planning and teaching.

Each school will have targets relating to achievement which they need to address; these will inform targets set for each class or year group and similarly each child will have targets to address. All this is in order to raise standards and levels of achievement. It is easy to forget that progress in literacy is not always quantifiable and is usually determined by context and purpose.

2010 Tuesday 29th June

WALT: ⊕ #L Write a story opening and build up.

*I n Prt IN THE ART GALLERY
Elizabeth, BSA

where
are they?
setting?

Georgia was walking with her twin sister, Jenny. They were both 18 and they looked exactly the same and wore denim dungarees. Georgia wore a pink Tshirt underneath while Jenny wore a blue Tshirt underneath.

excellent
description
of characters

Super
build-up.

They were going the Art Gallery. When they got there. Georgia took one look at the old building with crumbling walls and moaned: "Boring". "Whatever" was Jenny's answer. They entered the building. Georgia fell asleep halfway through the exhibit only to be woken up an hour later by Jenny dragging her across the soft carpet of

Super
metaphor.

the Art Gallery towards a golden framed picture. "Look" said Jenny. There. in front of them was the spooky picture of Professor Atlas. He had wild hair as red as fire, ruby beady eyes that hypnotized you instantly.
"Freaky" muttered Georgia.
"OK lets go home now" said Jenny nervously.

Just then. the "picture" winked at them.

"AAAAAA RRR G HHH!" screamed Jenny. waving her arms in the air and running for her life.
"Calm down Jenny" said Georgia, staring blankly at the ugly picture.

Leila, this is a fabulous start to your story. well done!

(Continues)

(Continued)

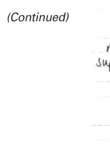

Figure 6.8 Opening of an adventure story written by Leila, aged seven

Assessment of writing development

In spite of all that has been said above, it is important that teachers are able to look at children's writing and to respond to it, showing them how they can improve as writers.

Figure 6.8 shows the start of Leila's adventure story, called 'In the Art Gallery'. Leila was in Year 3 (age 7–8) and this adventure story was written at the end of a unit of work. The unit of work is discussed in Chapter 7. Look first at Leila's writing.

> **Comment**
>
> Identify all the things that Leila has demonstrated she is able to do in this piece of writing.
>
> She introduced the characters giving full descriptions of their physical appearance. She used direct speech effectively to convey the mood of the characters. She used complex sentence structures. The words she used were powerful and evocative and she also used metaphor and simile. She is able to use punctuation to add meaning, for example when she puts 'picture' in inverted commas.

This is a good piece of writing which creates the appropriate effect of an adventure story on the audience. How would you respond to the start of that story as a reader? When I read it, I wanted to know if the twins were alike in character as well as appearance; I wanted to know why they were going to the art gallery; I wanted to know why Georgia fell asleep. If I were Leila's teacher I would want to talk to her about those questions I have as a reader and help her to see how they can help her as a writer to improve her writing. Once a writer has decided on the effect that is required through the writing, then the decision can be made about vocabulary choice, sentence structure and imagery.

Figure 6.9 shows how Leila was encouraged to assess her own writing. The class had together constructed an 'Adventure Story checklist' which was derived from their reading and analysis of adventure stories. The children evaluated their own work against this, as did the teacher.

Adventure Story Checklist

Pupil	Have I included ...	Teacher
✓ ☺	**Opening:** I introduced the characters	✓
	I gave information about the characters	✓
	I used adjectives	✓
	Build-up: I used powerful verbs	✓
	I described the setting using senses	
	I started my sentences using adverbs to build suspense!	
	I have used imagery: simile and metaphor	✓
	I used short sentences	✓
	Climax/Problem: I used time connectives to move the story on	✓
☺✓	I used speech to show the reader about the characters	✓
～☺	I resolved the suspense from previous chapter	
	I used long sentences to slow the pace	
✓ ☺	**Story Resolution:** I have included 'help' arriving unexpectedly	✓
☺✓	I have described the character's reaction	✓
	I have used powerful verbs and connectives	✓
	Story Ending: I have included my characters going home	
	I have used speech or what the character is thinking to show whether they have learned their lesson	
	What could I do to improve my work next time?	

Figure 6.9 Checklist for writing an adventure story created by a class of 7- to- 8-year-olds and used by them to evaluate their own writing

> **Task**
> Look carefully at Leila's writing and the checklist and decide what writing targets you would give her if you were her teacher.

OBSERVATION: Story written by a Year 1 child (age 5)

Figure 6.10 is another example of writing by a younger child. It reads,

I was going to school on the way a TRex took my school bag I threw my shal at the TRex Veronica you are late go and write 300 tim I must not tell lise

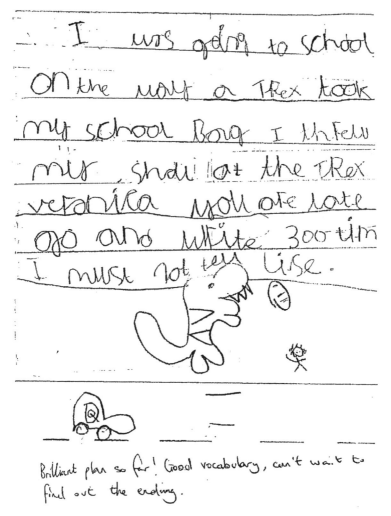

Figure 6.10 Story written by a 5-year-old

Comment

It is always best to identify first what a child is able to do. This child:

- writes in sentences
- uses direct speech
- uses verb tenses appropriately
- spells most words in a phonically consistent way
- structures a story clearly with a beginning, middle and end.

There are clear areas for development in relation to transcriptional skills: demarcation of sentences with capital letters and full stops, demarcation of direct speech and the use of adjectives to increase detail in description.

Task

What would you say to this child about her writing? How would you respond as a reader? How would this support the child in improving her writing?

What have we learned about assessment of writing?

- Effective writing can best be judged by its 'fitness for purpose'.
- Assessing writing should involve some consideration of the process and cannot always be done thoroughly by focusing just on the product.
- Good transcriptional skills do not necessarily mean good compositional skills and vice versa.
- Quality of writing often depends on what is being written.

Assessment of reading development

When looking at progress in reading the simple view of reading is a useful reminder of the key elements. An effective reader will be good in both word identification and language comprehension. However, it is not always as simple as that and reading is a much more complex process than that statement might suggest. In assessing reading development, teachers need the skill of looking and listening to all that children say and do not say, and making judgements, based on their understanding of what reading is.

> **Read**
>
> Goswami, U. (2008) 'Reading, complexity and the brain', *Literacy*, 42(2): 67–74.
>
> Harrison, C. (2010) *Interdisciplinary Perspectives on Learning to Read.* London: Taylor and Francis.
>
> These two texts will give you an introduction to all the different research perspectives which are used to understand the reading process and what they have to offer us as teachers.

One very useful strategy for assessing reading is 'miscue analysis' or 'running record'. This was first devised by Ken Goodman in the 1970s and involves listening carefully to a child reading an unknown text and noting what is said when 'errors' or 'miscues' are made. This can indicate to you what knowledge the child is drawing on when reading and so indicate future teaching that needs to be done. What follows is an example of such an assessment of an individual child's reading.

OBSERVATION: Reading of a Year 1 child (age 6)

The teacher listened to the child read aloud and recorded everything the child said. The child was given as little help as possible so that the teacher could identify the degree of independence as a reader and the strategies the child used to work out an unknown word.

> **Comment**
>
> Children need to be independent and have a variety of problem solving strategies at their disposal when they come across an unknown word. This is the basis of independent reading. The knowledge of strategies used by a child will inform the teacher of the teaching and scaffolding the child needs in subsequent shared and guided reading sessions.

The first 'error' the child made was when attempting to read the word 'said' in the sentence, 'Mum said, come in the car, Nick'. The child attempted to sound out the word using single phoneme–grapheme correspondences. This lead to /s//a//i/; at this point the child realised that it was a vowel digraph and read the word as, 'say'. It appeared as though the effort of working out the phonemic structure of the word was such that once a recognisable word was reached the child was content! She then started reading again from the beginning of the page, realised that 'Mum say ...' did not make sense, saw the/d/ and self-corrected to read, 'Mum said ...'.

> **Comment**
> The first strategy used for decoding the word was phonics. The child was confident in simple phoneme–grapheme correspondences but less so when it came to vowel diagraphs. It was rereading and using the meaning of the sentence that enabled the child to realise the decoded word did not make sense, to self-correct and eventually to get to the correct word. This example emphasises the importance of phonics in tackling unknown words but also that it is not enough on its own. If this child's ear was not tuned in to the sense of what she was reading she would not have realised that what she said did not make sense. She would have learned this from her experiences from read-aloud sessions, shared reading and guided reading.

The next 'error' made followed a similar pattern. The text on the page was, '"Here I come," said Nick.' The child read 'Her I come'. This shows that again it was the vowel phoneme which was causing this child difficulties. She recognised the capital 'h' and decoded using simple phoneme–grapheme correspondences/h//er/, failing to notice that the word actually contains a split digraph.

> **Comment**
> A pattern is beginning to emerge in this child's reading. She again self-corrected when she realised that her first decoding attempt did not make sense. She used the meaning of the text to inform her. Do you think this is a positive reading strategy adopted by this child?

As the child read on she began to relate more to the sense of the text, making comments on it as she read. These comments often referred to the illustrations: 'He looks scared.' The text was a very basic text and did not offer much in terms of subtlety of meaning. The child was making more meaning by referring to the illustrations and also by relating the text to her own experiences. After reading the sentence, 'Here is Teddy' she commented, 'I've got a teddy bear too'.

> **Comment**
> It is clear that while using phonics as a key strategy for decoding the child is also drawing on her experiences of life and her knowledge that texts usually make sense to read this book. How does this relate to what you already know about the reading process?

The final 'error' the child makes is on the very last page. The book has a large illustration of a little boy hugging a very large teddy bear. The words are, 'Teddy is in the car too'. The child spent a long time looking at the illustration and then read 'Bear is in the car too'. She then stopped and said, 'No, not a bear. His name is Teddy'.

Comment

Here we have evidence of the meaning of the text having priority in the mind of the child. She was drawing on her knowledge of the text so far and relating it very closely to her own experiences of life. It seems that it was her prior knowledge of the text that caused her to self-correct here and not her phonic knowledge, although it is clear that she would have been able to decode that word. What does this tell you about the process of learning to read?

An overall analysis of this child's reading would indicate that she has a growing confidence in reading and is able both to recognise high-frequency words and relate what she reads to her own personal experiences. She has a sound grasp of simple phoneme to grapheme correspondences but is not so confident with more complex vowel phonemes. She tends to look only at the first part of a word when blending the phonemes and does not blend throughout the whole word. She recognises when she has misread and will usually self-correct. She made a personal response to the text, relating it to her own experiences.

Comment

What would you say were the priorities for teaching with this child? Consider discrete phonic teaching and also the teaching of reading in its broadest sense. Identify some of the things you would do if you were this child's teacher.

The analysis of a child's reading in this way gives teachers many pointers to future teaching. Of course, it cannot (and should not) be done on a daily basis but done regularly and systematically will inform teachers' planning to enable it to be more focused and appropriate to individual needs.

With older children it is helpful as a strategy to identify the needs of struggling readers in particular and our next observation is of a Year 4 child.

OBSERVATION: Reading of a Year 4 child (age 9)

Conor was reading a quite challenging text which was an extract of an account of the ascent of Everest written by Sir John Hunt. The table in Figure 6.11 indicates the errors he made.

	Actual text	What was read
1	rarefied	rare – fied
2	on	in
3	now	so
4	on	to (then self-corrected)
5	regimen	regg – ee – men
6	acclimatisation	ak – lee – matisation
7	best	bad
8	provided	prov – prov – provided
9	gradualness	gra – grad – gradual – gradualness
10	detriment	de – try – ment
11	make	take
12	too far	far too

Figure 6.11 Errors made by a 9-year-old child when reading aloud

These are the errors made in the first two paragraphs of the text – 12 errors from 160 words. That makes an error rate of 7.5 per cent. This does not take into account the long pauses in his reading which were also recorded. The rest of the text consists of 179 words and there are 14 errors. This gives an error rate of 7.7 per cent over the whole passage.

Think about

What does this tell you about the suitability of the text for this child?

This was clearly a challenging text for this child and many of the words with which he struggled were difficult words. It is doubtful that he would be able to understand the full meaning of the text as he would not be fully engaged with it. Let us look at some of his 'miscues' in detail.

Error number 2 is with the word 'rarefied'. It is doubtful that Conor had heard of this word before. Notice that he first breaks it into two syllables. This indicates that he does not know the word as it actually has three syllables.

Error number 5 is a demonstration of Conor's phonic knowledge. What does it tell us?

- He could break the word into three syllables.
- He knows that the grapheme 'i' can sometimes represent the phoneme /ee/.
- He knows that the grapheme 'g' represents the phoneme /g/.
- He probably does not understand what the word 'regimen' means and it is likely that he has never heard it spoken or read.

In the light of all this, Conor has made a good attempt at reading this word. The same can be said for many of the other attempts he has made to segment words and use his phonic knowledge to read them. Look at these 'miscues' and try to identify the strategies Conor used.

> **Think**
>
> What does this example of Conor's knowledge tell you about him as a reader?

An overview of Conor's reading shows a mixed approach to word identification. There are times when he skilfully identified the phonemes in a word and blended them to read the word correctly. There are other times when he made basic phonic errors and other times when he reversed the order of the words. This pattern of miscues seems to emphasise the difficulty of the text for Conor; it appears that the level of challenge was such that, in his attempt to make sense of this rather obscure passage, he was unable to rely on decoding skills. Even when he could decode a word he did not understand it and this hampered his understanding of the whole text.

What have we learned about assessment of reading?

- Assessing reading needs to take account of the text that is being read and how suitable it is for the reader.
- Assessing reading needs to focus on the growing independence of the reader.
- Assessing reading should focus on the strategies that are used to read unknown words.
- Quality of reading depends on quality of text.
- Assessing reading should consider word reading skills and also levels of comprehension and the pleasure gained from reading.

OBSERVATION: Reading journals

In one Year 5 class lots of volunteer helpers come in and spend time reading with individual children (age 9–10).

The teacher reads aloud to the children, talks with them about texts, does shared reading with the whole class and guided reading with groups but does not often hear individual children read aloud to him. He does, however, encourage children to read to volunteer helpers as often as possible.

> **Think**
>
> Why does the teacher himself not hear individual children read?
>
> Why does he encourage them to read to volunteer helpers?

You may have come up with several thoughts on these questions. It is helpful to consider what the teacher is in the classroom to do. It might sound really obvious but the main role of the teacher is to teach! This is done through all those activities listed above. The purpose of reading aloud is either to assess individual achievements or to give opportunity for children to practise the skills they have learned.

In this classroom the teacher keeps a large book in which everyone who hears a child reads records what they have heard. Here are a few examples.

There are four different handwriting styles in Maisy's reading journal – her mother, her father, the teaching assistant and a volunteer parent.

21/9 – Work on expression and spotting punctuation. Read very well. 'creatures, people, rocket, climbed, spacesuit'

27/9 – self-correcting, needs to try to blend eg cl br but she read well

28/9 – finished book. She corrected herself but got stuck on the word 'thought'. She kept saying 'thinking'

24/10 – 'Underground Adventure' – finished book making very few mistakes, self-correcting if necessary. However got very stuck on 'visit' – could not blend it.

> **Comment**
>
> It seems evident from these comments that Maisy reads with understanding. She reads with expression, using the punctuation. Remember that punctuation is there for the reader and it can sometimes be fun with Key Stage 2 children to change the punctuation in a passage and see how it would change the way in which you read it.
>
> Maisy also self-corrects. This implies that she is listening to what she reads and notices if it does not make sense.

> She is having some difficulty blending some words. Why do you think she struggled with 'visit' but coped well with 'people'?

Benjamin:

28/4 – tried very hard but kept on getting the word 'origin' wrong and made some silly errors
18/10 – good reading/decoding. Crumpled/staggered/pathetically Should see some of this great language in Ben's writing
24/11 – good reading – must make sure he stays on a coloured banded book – really check if only decoding or comprehending. Keep an eye on punctuation.

Look at the comment made about Benjamin's reading on 24/11. He seems to be reading well but the person listening is not sure that he is really comprehending the text or just has good decoding skills. There is a hint that he is not using the punctuation in his reading and so it lacks fluency.

Comment
How would you respond to this if you were Benjamin's teacher? Relate these comments to the simple view of reading which stresses the importance of the relationship between word recognition and language comprehension. The aim is that children are in the quartile where both are good. What sort of questions would you want to ask Benjamin about a text to ensure that he is really comprehending what he is reading? Remember you do not want to monitor his recall but to evaluate his understanding of the essential meaning of the text.

In addition to this ongoing assessment the class used a sentence-based reading test as a way of tracking progression over the year. This can be a useful way of measuring progress but be careful that you always bear in mind the holistic nature of the reading process and do not think you are assessing reading when you are only assessing one aspect of it.

Principles of assessment in literacy

One of the key influences on thinking and practice in assessment has been the work of Shirley Clarke and much of her thinking can be seen implemented in primary classrooms. She has listed seven key strategies involved in formative assessment (Clarke 2008: 11) and, in concluding this chapter, it is worth considering them with specific reference to literacy.

1. *Creating a classroom culture in which all involved see ability as incremental rather than fixed.* This means that there is no standard way in which all children will develop and achieve. What it means to improve as a reader and a writer will be different for each child and will depend on the text, the social and cultural context of the literacy learning and the purpose and relevance of the learning event.

2. *Involving pupils in planning both appropriately pitched content and meaningful contexts.* Literacy is highly dependent on the social and cultural context and children need to understand the function and relevance of literacy, if they are to succeed in becoming literate. For many children what being literate means in school will be very different from what being literate means at home. Children will be more successful if they feel comfortable with the literacy experiences offered to them and are also able to make decisions about the literacies they use.

3. *Clarifying learning objectives and establishing pupil-generated and therefore pupil-owned success criteria.* We saw this in practice when we looked at Leila's writing and the success criteria which had been generated by the reading and analysis of texts. This meant that the criteria were fully understood by Leila and her classmates because they could relate them specifically to texts they had read and so knew what it looked like in concrete terms. They used language they understood to create them and understood why these ideas would make their writing better.

4. *Enabling and planning effective classroom dialogic talk and worthwhile questioning.* Throughout this book the centrality of talk to the learning process has been emphasised. We know true learning has occurred when we can explain what we have learned to somebody else. Talk is a real indicator of learning. Teacher questions are important as a way of probing learning; questions which invite explanation and discussion provide evidence of deep learning rather than closed questions which invite repetition rather than re-creation.

5. *Involving pupils in analysis and discussion about what excellence consists of – not just the meeting of success criteria, but how to best meet them.* The development of a unit of work in literacy as we have described in this chapter gives many opportunities for children both to analyse and discuss what makes for a good text or piece of writing. By reflecting on how an author creates a particular effect, children are shown how to create that effect themselves.

6. *Enabling pupils to be effective self- and peer-evaluators.* The use of talk and/or response partners and the generation of success ladders are just some of the strategies which enable children to evaluate their own work. As a learner, you will be very aware that your work only really improves when you understand why it went wrong and how it can be changed to be made better. Children are no different.

7. *Establishing continual opportunities for timely review and feedback from teachers and pupils, focusing on recognition of success and improvement needs and provision of time to act on that feedback.* The process of becoming

a reader and writer is a complex one and requires time and practice. An effective literacy teacher will have the subject knowledge to be able to see what children are doing, to know what needs to come next and to create opportunities to extend and challenge learning. Monitoring learning is a continuous element of teaching and planning must be flexible and open to allow the children's needs to be addressed.

Read

Clarke, S. (2008) *Active Learning Through Formative Assessment*. London: Hodder Education.

Summary

The worst thing you can think about both planning and assessment is that they are both fixed practices which are done and dusted so that teachers can then move on to the real business of teaching. That is not the case at all. Both assessment and planning are ongoing and permeate the whole of that strange and complex business called teaching. They feed from each other and need to be both precise and yet open-ended at the same time. Planning cannot happen without assessment and, in a way, assessment depends on planning so that teachers know what to look for. However, both are concerned with children's learning. We plan to make a difference to children's knowledge, skills or understanding and we assess to see how that difference manifests itself.

Further reading

Paratore, J.R. and McCormack, R.L. (eds) (2007) *Classroom Literacy Assessment: Making Sense of What Students Know and Do*. New York: Guilford Press.

CHAPTER 7

TEACHING WITH STORY

This chapter explores the role of story within the curriculum and its impact on learning. The observations, across the primary age range, look at story through role play and oral storytelling as well as analysing stories in preparation for writing. It argues that story is an essential part of being human and working with story can enhance our understanding of both ourselves and the world in which we live.

What does 'story' mean? Spend some time thinking about what comes into your mind when you hear that word. The term 'story' can cover a whole range of texts, oral, visual and written. Traditional stories tend to be those which we consider to have originated in the oral tradition. They include myth, fable, legend, folk tale and others. Even in the twenty-first century, however, stories come in all forms. They can be written, drawn, told, acted and filmed. Stories are told, read or remembered fictional or factual accounts. There is a huge range of story types – sagas, anecdotes, dramas, to name but a few. If I were to ask for your favourite story, I am sure you would be able to name several. I am also sure that if I asked several people their favourite stories there would be many common ones identified. Telling stories is an essential element of what it means to be a human being and we all read, listen to and tell stories each day of our lives. Why is story so important in our lives?

- Story helps us to make sense of our experiences: by creating a story I am able to come to terms with events in my life. For example, several months ago when I drove into the back of the car in front of me, when telling the story about this to other people I emphasised the rain, the fading light, the busyness of the road with cars and pedestrians crossing in between cars and my tiredness at the end of a long day. It was this storytelling that made me feel better about what was clearly a mistake on my part and also generated sympathy in my listeners and made me feel better. I constructed a story to make sense of that rather unpleasant experience.
- Reading and hearing stories helps us to enter into experiences which might otherwise be outside our normal lives. This explains the popularity of romantic fiction, of spy thrillers and of crime detective novels. Story gives me vicarious experiences.
- It is these vicarious experiences that allow me to extend my understanding, my vocabulary and to explore my own values and beliefs. Story expands the database of experiences within which my cognitive development takes place.
- There is also a huge social and cultural aspect to story. I recently read *Toast* by Nigel Slater and his descriptions of the food of his childhood immediately took me straight back to my childhood and I could see and taste the food he was describing. Some stories reinforce social and cultural understandings and others broaden experiences and help readers and listeners understand the social norms of others.
- Story introduces readers and listeners to the rhythm and power of literary language. The first page of *Peace at Last* by Jill Murphy reads as 'The hour was late'. That is not the language that is used at bedtime in my house and I suspect not in yours, but it is literary language. It prepares the reader that something is going to happen and creates an atmosphere of wonder and anticipation.
- Stories introduce listeners and readers to huge concepts about the world – good and bad, honesty and deceit, poverty and wealth, kings and woodcutters. At the same time they consider the most intimate aspects of our lives – both personal and universal.

For these reasons, and others, stories have been the most powerful method of teaching since the beginning of history. Hardy (1977) famously described narrative as 'a primary act of mind', arguing that it is the way in which we make sense of our experiences. She wrote that we use story in our head ('inner storytelling') and told to other people ('outer storytelling') to make sense of our lives and the events in them. Story is central to understanding and learning and so should be central to our teaching.

In this chapter many of the observations focus on the written form of story but this is not to undervalue the importance of storying and storytelling. These two should have a place in the curriculum in their own right because of their impact on children's learning. Do not think that children move seamlessly from listening, telling or reading stories into writing. The place of story within the curriculum is more holistic than that.

Read

Grugeon, E. and Gardner, P. (2000) *The Art of Storytelling for Teachers and Pupils: Using Story to Develop Literacy in the Primary Classroom*. London: David Fulton.

Grainger, T. (1997) *Traditional Storytelling*. Leamington Spa: Scholastic.

OBSERVATION: Storytelling in a Year 1 class (ages 5 and 6)

One of the most important features of working with story is storytelling. It is difficult to capture this in an observation because often it is spontaneous and it is difficult to record everything that is said and the responses that are made. I watched a teacher tell a story to her Year 1 class after a very windy playtime. The story she told was very roughly based on Aesop's fable about the wind and the sun, where they try to find out who is the most powerful by attempting to make a traveller remove his coat. The children came into the classroom loudly; their hair was blown and their faces red. It had been very windy outside and they were talking loudly about how they had been blown about and had to chase scarves and so on across the playground. The teacher sent them to hang up their coats and come and sit down quickly because she knew a story which was exactly about what had happened during their playtime.

Comment

Instead of ignoring the children's excitement of the wind, the teacher harnessed this and used it to focus their attention. They immediately wanted to listen and become involved. She had used the 'hook' of their own experiences to draw them in.

When the children were settled, the teacher began telling them the story – but with a difference. She told a story about a class of children outside in the wind. The wind was trying hard to make them take off their coats and scarves and throw them away and wanted to make the children naughty. In telling the story, the teacher named every child in the class, picking up on what they had told her about their adventures outside.

> **Comment**
> The children quickly realised that this story was about them and once the first name was mentioned were carefully listening for their own name. They were hanging on her every word.

The story lasted for only about 5 minutes but at the end the children were quietly settled and ready to begin the next lesson. The teacher told them that there was a story very similar to 'theirs' and during the lunch hour she found a copy of the Aesop's fable, read it to them and put it on display in the book corner.

> **Comment**
> This was not a planned lesson and lasted for a very short time but it served three very powerful purposes. It calmed the children down and focused them back to the teacher and into a listening frame of mind. It introduced them to a traditional fable and motivated them to read that for themselves and go on to read other fables later. Lastly, it demonstrated to them the power and universality of story – linking an ancient story with their own very recent experience, helping them to make sense of both.

It is important to remember that much learning happens in the classroom that is unplanned. This was an experienced teacher and she had the confidence to take 5 minutes from the planned lesson. She also had the subject knowledge of Aesop's fable to be able to draw on that and use it to make the link with the children's immediate experiences.

OBSERVATION: Guided reading with an EAL group in Year R (ages 4 and 5)

The next observation is of a teacher reading with a Reception class. It was a guided reading lesson and she wanted to support them in making meaning from the text. The group of children had not been in school for long and the majority of them did not share the social and cultural background of the story. The teacher, therefore, wanted them to experience this in order to enhance their understanding. She did this through role play.

This lesson was with a group of six children who were at the start of their second term in school. They did not have much English. They were working with a teacher looking at a story called *Getting Up* by R. Hunt.

The lesson took the form of role play. The teacher took on all the roles and the children joined in with her, using the props and echoing her language. Props used included toothbrushes and toothpaste, coats and scarves, wellington boots, etc. The teacher turned to each page in the book and showed it to the group. She gave them some time to look at the picture before asking for comment.

Comment

Thinking time is important as we have already seen in preceding chapters. In this instance, it allowed the children to look carefully at the details of the pictures and to relate them to their own experiences. The frequent emphasis on pace and 'correct' answers can sometimes contradict what we know about how learning takes place through the co-construction of knowledge and understanding. The article cited below considers how the use of the interactive whiteboard (IWB) can support children's understanding and encourage the use of dialogic teaching. It is mainly about work with older children but as you read it consider the similarities and differences between how the IWB was used with 12–13-year-old pupils and how the reception teacher in our observation used role play for the same purpose.

Read

Mercer, N., Hennessy, S. and Warwick, P. (2010) 'Using interactive whiteboards to orchestrate classroom dialogue', *Technology, Pedagogy and Education*, 19(2): 195–209.

These children became part of the story in order to understand what was happening. They were able to use language in authentic situations and because they had experienced the scenario were able to tell the story. The lesson was recorded and the children returned to it many times, looking at the book and the video and retelling the story to each other.

OBSERVATION: Year 1 children (ages 5 and 6) retelling the story of *We're Going on a Bear Hunt*

The next observation is of a group of children in a Year 1 class during independent activity time. The class had been working on the text *We're Going on a Bear Hunt* by Michael Rosen and there were multiple copies of this in the book corner. Alongside this was a story sack related to this text.

Story sacks were originated by Neil Griffiths. A story sack is a cloth bag full of resources to encourage children and adults to enjoy reading together. The sack is based around a well-known picture story book and usually also includes a non-fiction book on a similar theme. There are also a variety of artefacts: soft toy characters, props and scenery and also a game, a CD of the story, an activity guide and a guide for parents.

This sack was rather unusual in that it contained a copy of the book and nothing else but some lengths of different types of material. There was a length of textured green linen, a length of patterned material in different shades of blue, a length of brown satin, a length of rough dark brown hessian, a length of white netting and, finally, a piece of heavy black cotton.

A group of children were sent to explore this resource during the independent time of a literacy lesson and told to prepare a storytelling for the rest of the class. A teaching assistant was supporting them. They began by opening the sack, taking out the material and waving it about.

Some of the material was more fluid than others and the children soon noticed it and commented to each other: 'This is like a flag.' 'This won't wave about – it's really heavy.' 'I can see through this.' 'I don't like the feel of this – it's scratchy.' They took about 5 minutes doing this, passing different materials from one to the other and comparing them.

> **Comment**
> At the beginning of this activity they had not even thought about the story which was the focus of their task. Do you think this was a waste of time? If not, what was the purpose of this part of the activity?

After several minutes of exploring and discussing the contents of the bag, the children had a good understanding of what each length of material was like and had developed a bank of strong descriptive words for talking about the materials. The teaching assistant then picked up the text and suggested they look at it. The children were very familiar with the text and so immediately began considering how to match the materials with the different settings in the story. They turned immediately to the coloured 'grass page' and did not bother to look at or read the pages before. One child immediately picked up the green material and waved it in the air while the whole group chanted, 'Swishy; swashy! Swishy, swashy! Swishy, swashy!'

The group worked through the book, looking just at the coloured pages and matching the lengths of materials to the pages. There was almost complete agreement except for the two brown lengths of material – the satin and the hessian. This was the only occasion that the decision was not based on colour alone. There was a heated discussion between the children.

Child 1:   I think this [the satin] is the forest because you can't see through it.
Child 2:   But it's shiny!
Child 1:   So are the trees [pointing to the trunks of the trees].
Child 3:   Well I think this [hessian] is better for the trees because it's prickly like all the twigs and branches
Child 2:   Hey look – don't you think this shiny stuff looks wet like the mud.
Child 3:   Oh yes, I never thought of that.
Child 1:   But you can't see through it.

Child 3:   I think the shiny stuff is best for the mud and the prickly stuff for the forest.

Child 2:   I'm happy with that. Let's go for it!

Child 1:   OK then.

> **Comment**
>
> There were at least two influences on this conversation. First, the children knew the story really well. They had had it read to them many many times and it had been in the book corner for them to read independently. They had also talked about the book in class and had discussed what it would be like to squelch through the mud and stumble through the forest; they had role-played the story and experienced those actions. Secondly, they had experienced and talked about the different materials. The relatively long time that they had spent 'playing' with the materials at the start of the activity was now bearing fruit because the children knew what each piece felt like and had a vocabulary to describe them. The judgements they were making to match the materials with the text were therefore informed decisions.

The teaching assistant then asked the children how they could use the material to tell the story to the rest of the class as instructed. They first said that they could just wave the materials in the air at the right time while somebody read the book but, when asked by the teaching assistant if they could make it even better, they began to think more closely about the text. They focused on the first page and identified the words 'over', 'under' and 'through'. Two children held an end of the blue material and another child stepped over it, then they moved it over that child and then one child let go of his end while the child walked through it. They got excited about this idea and looked through the book to check that each page was the same. When they found it was, they decided that two children would hold all the materials in turn while the other children would be the walkers and would 'tell' the story. This they did and the resulting 'performance' to the whole class was impressive.

> **Comment**
>
> Notice how the children's knowledge of the text modified what they did. They needed to be focused initially but once this had happened they took control and planned the whole thing themselves. They could do this because they possessed the required knowledge. This text had become part of the children's thinking because they had heard it and talked about it a lot. They knew the story and so were able to make it their own.

An approach to storytelling devised by Pie Corbett is described as 'Talk for Writing' to support children's writing of stories. It involves the children memorising a story through repeating the lines and linking them to actions and also works well as a family literacy activity. Corbett identifies three stages in the development of storytelling and argues that each stage must be fully internalised before moving on to the next. The three stages are:

- Imitation. This is where children listen and join in to stories, becoming very familiar with just a few so they can internalise the structures and linguistic patterns of the story. He suggests that during Reception and Year 1 (ages 4–6) teachers focus on just two to three stories a term, although the children will hear a range of quality stories in addition. The stories which become the focus of attention are repeated and learned.
- Innovation. When a story is well known then one or more aspects can be changed. These changes may range from the very simple, such as the name of a character, to the setting or to the resolution of the dilemma within the plot.
- Invention. Having spent time getting to know stories and playing with their structure, Corbett argues that children are ready then to create their own stories.

Read

More information about this can be found in the DCSF publication of 2008 called *Talk for Writing*.

Comment

Relate Pie Corbett's model to the *We're Going on a Bear Hunt* activity described above. The children were clearly engaged in an 'imitation' activity However, the teacher and the children had not consciously learned the story, nor had they learned appropriate actions to go with the words. One could almost say that the book itself had enabled them to remember and repeat. The rhythm, rhyme and unforced repetition of the text lent itself to natural action. Can you think of any more stories for which this is the case? Look back to Chapter 1 and think again about what Margaret Meek and Vivienne Smith say about what texts teach readers.

It is interesting to put this strategy into a theoretical framework. In Chapter 4 we saw how Corbett's work is based on the developmental psycholinguist, Traute Taeschner, from Rome. Her work (Taeschner 1991) argued that language acquisition, particularly the acquisition of a second language, is about internalising the patterns of the language. Myhill and Jones (2010) have explored the theoretical underpinning further in relation particularly, to the idea of 'oral rehearsal'. They found that there was much confusion in policy, in strategy writing and in teachers' thinking about what oral rehearsal actually is.

Myhill and Jones's research looked at how oral rehearsal is used in early years' classrooms. They found that there is no clear theoretical conceptualisation of what it is and indeed, the guidance in policy documents is often contradictory. However, they did find that it seemed to have a positive impact on children's writing.

Read

Myhill, D. and Jones, S. (2010) 'How talk becomes text: investigating the concept of oral rehearsal in early years' classrooms', *British Journal of Educational Studies*, 57(3): 265–84.

As Pie Corbett argues, it is true that all stories have the same basic structure and familiarity with that structure helps children in their own writing. When planning a unit of work in literacy it is important that children first have lots of experience of the type of text they are going to write and have spent time talking about it and looking at specific texts to draw out key features. The process can be described as a series of over-lapping circles which you will see if you look in the *Talk for Writing* publication (DCSF 2008).

The essential stages of the writing process which need to be taken into account when planning a unit of work are:

- familiarisation with text type
- capturing ideas
- teacher demonstration
- independent writing.

They build upon each other and so it is important that each stage is given enough time before moving on to the next. The following observation shows how this works in practice.

OBSERVATION: Unit of work on adventure stories with Year 3 class (ages 7 and 8)

The unit of work described here lasted for five sessions, taking place on consecutive days over a week. It was the precursor of work the following week where the children wrote their own adventure stories.

Lesson 1

The first lesson began with the teacher asking the children what 'adventure' means. They suggested words such as exciting, funny, scary, unusual, which she recorded on the whiteboard. She then reminded them of books they had read recently, both as a class and as individuals and related those words and ideas to the books the children knew. This led to some more words being added to the list.

> **Comment**
>
> The teacher was starting this unit with the children's own ideas and under-standings. This activity was a way for the teacher to review the children's existing knowledge and understanding and so establish a firm basis for future work.

The teacher then showed the children the cover of the book *Gorilla* by Anthony Browne. They knew this book well as they had done some focused work on it in Year 2 and it was also a popular text for independent reading.

> **Comment**
>
> A well-known text was chosen because that allowed the teacher to direct the children's attention to selected features of the text. They had already made their own personal affective responses to the text and were familiar with the outline of the plot. This enabled the teacher to move them on in analysis of the text.

The teacher read the story to the class and, with her encouragement, they joined in and became involved. The teacher then explained that many stories have the same structure and showed them a visual way of describing this structure using the analogy of a mountain. The structure starts at the bottom of one side of the mountain with the 'opening', setting the scene and introducing the characters. Moving up the slope of the mountain, the 'build-up' creates the possibility of tension or a problem. At the top of the mountain the 'dilemma' manifests itself and as we descend the other side we move towards a 'resolution'. Reaching the flat land on the other side of the mountain the story comes to a satisfactory 'ending'.

The class were told to work with a talking partner and decide what the problem in this story was. There was much animated discussion and when each group had come to a decision ideas were shared with the whole class. Not all had come to the same conclusion; some thought it was that Hannah was lonely, some thought that it was the fact that her Father was too busy and spent too much time at work and others thought it was that the Gorilla gift was not what she wanted. All ideas were listened to and accepted but each group was required to justify their answers by referring to the text.

> **Comment**
>
> The teacher was showing here that all ideas are valid but that it is important to be able to justify an answer by referring to the text. This meant that the children were engaged in really close reading of the text – reading what was actually said not only through words but also in the illustrations, using the skills of inference and deduction.

The children were then given a task to complete in pairs. They had to use the story mountain structure and decide which parts of the story fitted into the different stages. Each pair had a copy of the text and had to put sticky notes where they thought each stage was. They had to agree as a pair and be able to justify their decisions. The teacher emphasised that there was no one correct answer and so it was important for each pair to be able to explain to others how they had come to their answer. They then came together in groups of six (three pairs) to compare and explain their decision.

Comment

This activity emphasises the importance of talk. At the end of the lesson there was no written work but the evidence of learning was in the explanations and justifications that the children shared with the class. This activity required them to become immersed in the text and to articulate their own personal understanding of it to others who might hold a different view.

After the class had compared their views each group was given a section of the story to demonstrate through freeze frame.

Comment

Freeze frame is a drama technique in which children take a particular scene or incident in a book and form a freeze frame or 'tableau' of the situation. This requires the children to think about the relationship of the characters to each other, body language and facial expression. A further development is that the teacher will ask different characters in the frame to say what they are thinking at that moment in time.

Read

Baldwin, P. and Fleming, K. (2003) *Teaching Literacy Through Drama: Creative Approaches*. London: Routledge.

The lesson ended by referring back to the list of words describing adventure stories. These were read as a class and the children were asked to relate them to the text of *Gorilla*. Some extra words were added and the lesson finished with the teacher telling the children that they would look at the book again in more detail in the next lesson.

Reflect

How do you think this lesson had begun to prepare the children for writing adventure stories?

Lesson 2

The second lesson began with a recap of the stages of a story:

- opening which introduces characters and setting
- a problem or a dilemma
- resolution of the dilemma
- ending.

The teacher then returned to the text of *Gorilla* and asked the children to name the characters in the book. The focus moved to Hannah and the children were told they were going to act as detectives and find out what kind of person Hannah was. They would have to hunt through the text for clues. This was done as a shared reading activity.

> **Comment**
> By setting up this as a problem solving activity the children were immediately engaged. The teacher could have said, 'I want you to write a description of Hannah and support what you say by examples from the text.' What difference would this make to how the children tackled the text?

The teacher then modelled the activity by looking at the first page together. The first sentence on the page said, 'Hannah loved gorillas'. The teacher explained how it was easy to discover something about Hannah from that sentence and the children nodded wisely. She then asked if they could discover anything more about Hannah from the first page. A few children commented that she was lonely. When asked to justify this most of the children referred to the illustration which shows Hannah sitting on her own reading a book and looking rather sad. The children commented on the fact that she was by herself and that her facial expression was sad. The teacher then asked the children to read the second paragraph on the page. This says, 'Her father didn't have time to take her to see one at the zoo. He didn't have time for anything.'

The teacher explained that hunting for clues in the text means also looking for what we can guess from what people say. The children then discussed how Hannah might be lonely because her father was so busy.

> **Comment**
> When we read our understanding of a text often comes through what is implied rather then what is directly said; in other words we are often reading 'between the lines'. This is known as inferential reading and relates to the ability to deduce ideas which are not in the text explicitly. It is an important aspect of learning to become a reader. Teachers can teach this skill by the questions they ask.

Read
Zucker, T.A., Justice, S.B. and Piasta, S.B. (2010) 'Preschool teachers' literal and inferential questions and children's responses during whole-class shared reading', *Early Childhood Research Quarterly*, 25(1): 65–83.

The class then went through the book looking for clues about Hannah and how she was feeling. By her questions, the teacher encouraged them to read inferentially and to look at both the words and the illustrations for clues.

The next task required the children to work in pairs, looking at copies of the text. They had to think about the father and list adjectives describing him on their individual whiteboards. Each pair came up with a good list of adjectives, having used both the words and the illustrations. The teacher then sent the children off to work independently. The core and lower ability groups were asked to create a list of adjectives describing the gorilla and then to use these adjectives to write a character description of the gorilla. The higher ability groups were asked to create a list of adjectives for both the gorilla and the father and then to write a comparison of the two characters. The children were asked to share their ideas as they worked.

Comment
Look at how the teacher initially supports the children. First, she was structuring the reading very closely by directing their attention to particular parts of the text and by her questioning focusing their thinking. Secondly, she gave them a framework for writing a character description: read the text closely, identify key words and then write the description. Lastly, she asked them to do the same thing independently, challenging the more able by introducing the idea of comparison.

Lesson 3

The third lesson continued to focus on the aspect of character within story structure but the learning objective was to introduce the idea of empathy or seeing things through the eyes of somebody else. The lesson began with the class sitting on the carpet and the teacher gave examples of real-life situations, asking the children if they could understand how people were feeling. The examples started with Theo Walcott not being selected to play for England and this immediately got the boys engaged and talking energetically about how he must have felt. A variety of examples were given which involved the whole class and after much talk the teacher introduced the word 'empathy', explaining that this is what happens when we understand what somebody is feeling.

> **Comment**
>
> Notice how the teacher started with the examples that were relevant and meaningful to the children. She gave them the opportunity to talk about events which were important to them first and that allowed them to experience empathy first hand. She then gave them the term to describe what they had already felt and discussed and so the new word was useful to them and so more likely to be remembered and used.

The teacher then turned to another book by Anthony Browne called *The Tunnel*. She read the story to the children up to the point where Rose has to decide whether or not to go through the tunnel. If you do not know this book already, go and read it before you carry on reading this observation. It is an established children's text and should be in your repertoire.

> **Read**
>
> Browne, A. (1997) *The Tunnel*. London: Walker Books.

The teacher stopped and said to the class, 'Rose faces a dilemma here. What is it?' There followed a discussion about Rose's situation. The teacher asked questions such as:

- What choices does Rose have?
- What thoughts do you think might be going through her head?
- Can you empathise with her?

The children worked in talk partners and came up with many different suggestions of what Rose might be thinking. The class then came together to share ideas. Children were asked to share what their talk partner had said rather than their own ideas.

> **Comment**
>
> Why do you think the teacher asked the children to report back on their partner's ideas and not their own? It is much easier to report on what somebody else has said in a public domain than to risk exposing one's own ideas. It also means that the children have to actively listen to what their partner is saying in order to be able to repeat it. It is often a good idea while they are learning to do this to get the children to repeat back to their talk partner what they are going to say.

The ideas shared by the children varied from, 'There might be something dangerous in there' to 'What if my brother needs help?' After hearing all the thoughts the teacher asked each person to decide if the thought they had expressed would lead Rose to go into the tunnel or stay outside. Again, they discussed this with their talk partner. The children were then asked to stand in two lines facing each other; one side was people for going into the tunnel and the other of people against going into the tunnel. The teacher was then Rose and walked between the two lines while the children whispered their comments to her, acting as her conscience.

Comment

'Conscience alley' is sometimes known as 'decision alley' or 'thought tunnel' and is a way of exploring the dilemma faced by a character. Those on one side of the tunnel give the opposing point of view from those on the other. It can be used in any area of the curriculum. On a practical note, it is a good idea to make sure the tunnel is quite wide; the children can sometimes become too enthusiastic and overpower the person walking through the tunnel. This is especially important if that person is a child. Note also that the children whispered their views. The children need to be reminded that it is not a case of who can shout the loudest in order to convince but is a demonstration of the debate that is going on in the mind. Drama can be a very powerful teaching tool as it allows children to experience the feelings of protagonists in any situation and so understand them more deeply.

This was a moving experience for the children and served to enhance their understanding both of what a dilemma was and also what it felt like to experience a dilemma. The teacher emphasised that having walked through the tunnel and listened to all the different points of view, Rose could now make a decision. She informed the class that Rose had decided not to go through the tunnel. Some of the children were clearly and vocally disappointed, an indication that they were fully engaged and empathised with Rose's dilemma. They were told that Rose was going to write a note to Jack and leave it under a stone outside the tunnel, explaining why she did not follow him. The children were given roughly torn scraps of paper on which to write their notes.

Comment

Why do you think the teacher gave them paper like that on which to write? How would it increase the quality of their writing? It certainly would have continued the sense of being in role; Rose would not have had an English exercise book with her and in such a situation would not have written the date and title neatly underlined! The teacher was consciously giving the children an authentic writing experience and this is an important thing to remember when planning.

When the writing was completed the children folded up their notes and placed them under large stones put around the classroom. The role play was continuing and it was the experience of the whole context of the lesson which enabled the children to achieve the learning objective of understanding what empathy is and being able to empathise with a character in a story.

The class then gathered for the plenary and one child was chosen to be Rose; another child was chosen to be a police officer. The teacher explained that Jack had never reappeared and Rose was being questioned later in her home about what had happened. This worked really well; the police officer was a little self-conscious at first but soon became more comfortable in his role and was quite perceptive and scary in his questioning. The girls in role as Rose answered the questions well, showing that they fully understood Rose's position.

> **Comment**
> The plenary was not used as a show-and-tell activity where children can easily get very bored by looking at lots of examples of the same thing. Instead the teacher went back to the learning objective and devised another activity which explored the children's understanding. All the children were involved as they began by suggesting what the police officers might ask and evaluated the responses given by Rose. Right to the very end of the lesson, the class was engaged and enthusiastic.

Lesson 4

This lesson began with the teacher finishing reading *The Tunnel* to the class. After the reading, she referred back to the story structure which she had introduced to the class through the use of the 'story mountain' in the first lesson. Through fairly direct questioning, she asked the children to identify the characters, the problem and the adventure in the story. The first two questions were answered quickly and without debate as they were reviewing prior learning but the third led to more debate. The question asked was, 'Where do you think the adventure began in the story?'

> **Comment**
> Note how the teacher was asking for the children's opinion. There was no sense that there was only one correct answer and the children were required to draw on their generic knowledge of adventure stories and their specific knowledge of this text to answer. This type of questioning continued right through the first part of the lesson.

There was a debate about whether the adventure began when Jack entered the tunnel or when Rose did, and the discussion involved lots of debate about what constituted an adventure. The children were then asked how they thought Jack got turned into stone. Again there were lots of ideas – ghosts, ice, evil spirits. The teacher referred the children back to the illustration for clues and they all felt that he looked as though he was running away from something or someone. Suggestions were made as to what that might be.

The children were then put into mixed-ability groups and asked to tell the story of what happened to Jack when he went through the tunnel by creating three freeze frames. The final of these was to be Jack being turned into stone; the first one was to be Jack emerging from the tunnel, showing what he saw and the middle one was completely up to the children. Before going off to work, the children were again shown the illustration in the book which showed Jack turned to stone. They were reminded that probably their final freeze frames would be quite similar but the first two could be very different.

Comment

Why do you think the groups for this activity were mixed ability? What would be the advantage of this? A 'freeze frame' is like a still image from a drama, when the characters freeze. It enables exploration of relative positioning, body language and expression to help understanding what is happening in a text at a particular moment of time. This is sometimes known as 'thought tracking'.

The children then watched each others' freeze frames and discussed the different view points.

Lesson 5

The fifth lesson was a shorter lesson at the end of the first week which summed up what the children had learned about adventure stories during the week before they began to start planning their own adventure stories. It began with a recap of the two books by Antony Browne that the class had worked on. The teacher used the discussion to draw up a list of the features of an adventure story, taking suggestions from the children. The focus in this lesson had gradually shifted from looking at setting, character and plot to considering how language was used to convey a sense of adventure. The final list contained the following features:

- Written in first or third person.
- Written in past tense with occasional switch to the present tense.
- The main characters tend to be human.
- The setting is linked to the adventure – being lost, at night, in a nightmare.
- Use of time connectives – early that morning, later on.
- Connectives to gain attention used – meanwhile, at that very moment.
- Connective to establish suspense used – suddenly, without warning.
- Speech and dialogue used.

- Verbs used to describe actions, thoughts and feelings.
- Vocabulary was chosen to give impact – adverbs, adjectives, expressive verbs, precise nouns, metaphors and similes.

Comment

All the items on this list were from suggestions by the children. Are you confident in your own subject knowledge that you could identify and discuss these features, giving examples from texts? The teacher used this list as the basis for a check list for evaluation of children's writing. See Figure 6.9 in Chapter 6.

The children were then sent to sit at their tables on which were placed a selection of different adventure stories; some were known to them and some were not. They spent time looking through them and searching for examples of the features identified above. In the plenary they were asked to identify these examples and told that next week they would begin to write their own adventure stories.

Comment

The five lessons which began this unit were designed to help children understand the features of a particular story type. If you look back at the lessons you will see that there was not much writing – this is not what the lessons were about. Go back to the beginning of the chapter and reflect on how the children had learned about story.

In this chapter on story we have seen how story-making is an essential characteristic of our humanity and that putting things into the framework of a story can greatly enhance the learning potential. Stories have been used for centuries to teach and convey cultural values and beliefs. Fables are an example of this kind of story and are often used as a focus for work in school. They are useful to study and write, primarily because they tend to be short! A fable is a story which usually features anthropomorphised animals or mythical creatures and which illustrates a moral lesson. The fable often ends with a short sharp sentence summing up the moral. The next observation looks at work focusing on fables.

OBSERVATION: Year 4 children writing fables (ages 8 and 9)

The class had already had experiences which had enabled them to become familiar with the characteristics of fables; they had read lots of fables both together and independently, and had discussed the special features of them. They were now ready to begin planning and writing their own fables. The teacher wanted this to be a short activity and so devoted just two lessons to this. Our observation focuses on the writing of one core ability boy in the class.

The first task was to list the features of a fable. Jo did this in his book:

- talking animals
- a moral
- pattern
- verbs
- adjectives.

He then wrote a heading 'Characters' and under that wrote: fox and lion.

The next heading was: What the fable is about (Figure 7.1). 'My fable is about a fox and a lion. The fox keeps on playing tricks on the lion. One day the lion invites the fox to tea.' He then wrote the moral of his fable: 'What goes around comes around.'

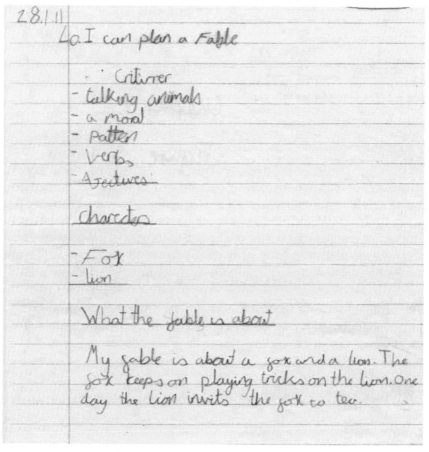

Figure 7.1 An 8-year-old plans a fable

Jo then planned his story in the form of a story map, as shown in Figure 7.2.

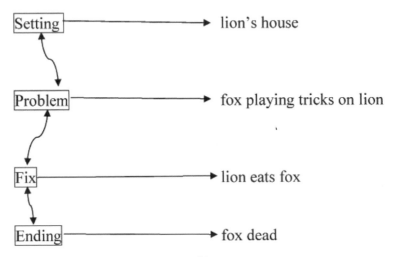

Figure 7.2 The plan of the story was turned into a story map

The planning took up the first lesson and the following lesson was devoted to independent writing work. Jo concentrated hard on writing his fable for the whole hour of the lesson and the first draft is reproduced in Figure 7.3.

In Figure 7.3 you can see the comments the teacher wrote on Jo's first draft. These comments were written with Jo as in the third lesson the teacher sat down with Jo and revised his work with him. The craft of writing is an important element of being a writer and it is a difficult one for children to learn. It is something that needs to be taught and can be modelled in shared writing and scaffolded in guided writing. The teacher looked at how Jo had written the direct speech in the first paragraph and helped him to see how it should be laid out on separate lines. This was a transcriptional error and one that could be easily rectified. Secondly, the teacher talked with Jo about the second paragraph. He read the paragraph to Jo and asked him to respond as a reader. As soon as he heard it read aloud Jo realised that it needed extra work and added two more sentences.

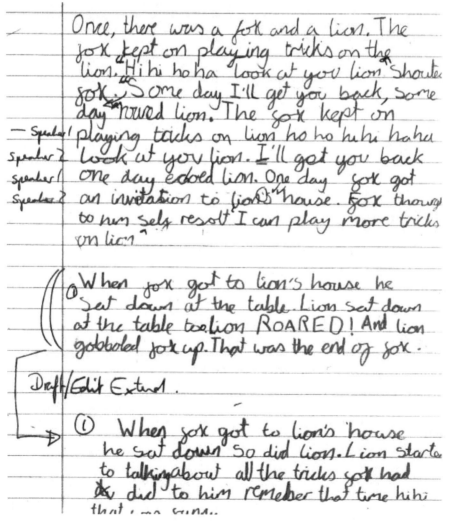

Figure 7.3 First draft of the fable with the teacher's responses and support for revision

> **Comment**
>
> Revising writing is a very challenging task for children, especially when focusing on compositional aspects. Jo, however, had been used to reading and analysing texts; he had been 'reading as a writer' and so this gave him the skills to do the same for his own writing. When reading texts with children, allow them first to respond as a reader and then to read as a writer.

> **Read**
>
> Barrs, M. and Cork, V. (2002) *The Reader in the Writer*. London: Centre for Language in Primary Education.

The last two observations have been concerned with children preparing to write stories. It is important to remember that this need not, indeed should not, always be the case. Story-making and storytelling can take place through a variety of media. We began by claiming that one value of story is that it helps us to see the world through somebody else's eyes, and this is what the next observation illustrates.

OBSERVATION: Year 5 children (ages 9 and 10) writing stories about Vikings

The class had been studying the Vikings in History and the class teacher wanted to give them an opportunity to demonstrate their understanding through story writing. He told them the story of the Viking raid on Danby. There was a lot of talk about what it was like for both the Vikings and the Saxons and how it felt for both sides to experience this raid first hand. Role play, talk and drama were among the teaching strategies used to help the children do this. The class first wrote stories about the raid as though they were a Saxon. This is Chris's story:

> *In the mist there was a large figure appearing from the sea. As it got closer and closer I could see a Viking boat! As it came closer I heard CHARGE! And they came towards us. The huge boat had a gigantic dragon face on the front, with the biggest sails I have ever seen! As I ran I saw fierce and tuff (sic) terrifying Vikings sprinting after me, Their faces were red with rage. I ran as fast as I could go. As I got home, I told my family, 'We have to run. Follow me!' We got to the point where we couldn't run any more and stopped but we were away from the Vikings.*

> **Comment**
> Look carefully at Chris's story and consider how writing it had given the teacher an insight into Chris's understanding of this Viking raid that writing a non-chronological account might not have done.

The next day the children were asked to write about the raid from the perspective of the Vikings. This is what Chris wrote:

> *I bellowed 'Charge!' We started to attack the Saxons. We were shocked at how many Saxons there were. They shouted, 'Ambush!' when I started to run at them. I knew they had been waiting anxiously for this day. There were metal swords flying up in the air and it felt terrifying. Red warm blood was spluttering out of cut and bruised bodies.*

> **Comment**
> Look carefully at both these stories and consider what they tell us about Chris and his understanding of story. He has written well from the different perspectives. Why do you think he talks about killing and death as a Viking but not as a Saxon? Why has he described the Viking boat as a Saxon but not as a Viking?

What we have not seen in this final observation is the preparation and work that went on before these stories were written. Chris could only write stories about this Viking invasion because he was familiar with the facts but also he had discussed what it would be like and had experienced it through drama. The story element of the work brought the history to life and deepened the children's understanding.

Booker (2004) argues that there are just seven basic plots to stories:

- overcoming the monster
- rags to riches
- the quest
- voyage and return
- comedy
- tragedy
- rebirth.

In looking at these plots we can see that, if Booker is correct, the whole gamut of human experience and emotion can be found and expressed in story. Bruner (2003) argues that we are all engaged in a self-making narrative through which we define and understand ourselves as we tell stories about our experiences. He argues that story gives us a particular kind of knowing;

we can 'know how' and 'know what' but we can only 'know what it is like' through story and that knowing enhances both understanding and our notion of self.

Summary

The observations in this chapter have, I hope, shown the importance and centrality of story in the learning process and how it can be included both in plans for teaching and in unplanned activities. In order to ensure that work on story is the most effective the following need to be part of our provision:

- providing access to a wide range of quality literature in all formats – oral, visual and written storytelling
- creating attractive displays that focus children's interests on story
- focusing on a writer or storyteller of the week or month
- selecting stories to record for other classes to develop children's storytelling skills
- working with writers and storytellers
- providing author boxes of books and lists of stories
- spreading enthusiasm by giving recommendations and encouraging children to share their favourites
- developing stories through drama and play.

It is through story that many children can find their way into learning and so we need to ensure that stories are at the heart of every subject on the curriculum.

Further reading

Ginnis, S. and Ginnis, P. (2006) *Covering the Curriculum with Stories: Six Cross-curricular Projects that Teach Literacy and Thinking through Dramatic Play.* Carmarthen: Crown House Publishing.

Daniel, K. (2011) *Storytelling Across the Primary Curriculum.* London: Routledge.

CHAPTER 8

TEACHING PRIMARY LITERACY

This concluding chapter considers all that has gone before in the journey towards becoming a teacher. What happens on that journey and how can we make it as smooth as possible?

There comes a time when the observing becomes less frequent and the teaching starts. Having said that, however, it is important to keep observing as much as possible. I have been teaching for a very long time but I still learn something every time I observe. Reflecting on what has been learned is essential, but that learning will have no value if it does not impact on practice. This concluding chapter draws together all the key features from previous chapters and puts them into the context of effective primary teaching.

Understanding texts

Our teaching must reflect the wide variety of texts that exist in society

Effective teaching of literacy means that we are enabling children both to read and create texts in a variety of different modes. Literacy as it is used in the twenty-first century is very different from even 20 years ago. I used to find it very difficult to compose directly onto a screen and am considering carefully whether or not buying an electronic reader will offer me the same experience as a book. My experiences do not count in teaching literacy; the world takes electronic communication in its stride and new developments happen daily. How is that reflected in the primary classroom?

It must mean that we use a range of texts in our teaching and we recognise the impact this will have on how we talk about texts. Electronic texts are often, but not always, predominantly visual and are rarely linear in construction. How do we teach children to read and create texts like that? It means that in our shared reading and writing texts like this are as usual as traditional paper-based texts and we are able to model and demonstrate the reading and writing process using these texts.

Texts must be at the heart of our planning

Teaching literacy is about teaching children to use different modes of communication to communicate and so they must be given experiences of these texts in the classroom. There has been an unfortunate tendency to use only extracts in teaching and this cannot effectively show children how texts work. I have known classes which have spent days reading lots of openings of books and stories and then writing several openings themselves without ever going on to read or write the continuation. I commend the children for their patience – I would find that experience very frustrating.

It is difficult, if planning is focused on skills, not to make your teaching very atomistic. If I am learning to write recipes, the best way is by reading lots of recipes and trying them out to see if they work. If they do work, consider why they work – what are the common features of successful recipes? I then need to write recipes and the test of my recipes will be if somebody can follow them and cook successfully what the recipe describes. The test of a good cake recipe is the end product of an edible cake and a calm cook. It is not how many time connectives or imperative verbs are used. The whole text is what is important.

The purposes of texts must be made clear and authentic texts used for genuine purposes

Unsworth argues that, 'In order to become effective participants in emerging multiliteracies, students need to understand how the resources of language, image and digital rhetorics can be deployed independently and interactively to construct different kinds of meanings. This means developing knowledge *about* linguistic, visual and digital meaning-making systems' (2001: 9). This means that literacy teaching must involve genuine experiences so that children understand the purposes of texts and can see how this works in practice. Letters and emails will be sent and responded to; notices will be put up to inform; instructions will be placed by the relevant object, stories will be shared and responded to. This means that discussions will be held about when it is more appropriate to write a letter than send an email, about whether a poster or a web page will reach more people with the information, about how the younger children will be most easily able to access the story.

Reading aloud to children

It is this element of literacy teaching that too frequently falls off the edge and it is easy to forget that reading aloud to children is actually a reading lesson and is a vitally important part of the curriculum. Make time to read to your children at least once every day and read them a variety of different types of texts. Try out new authors and new types of texts and reflect on them together. Use every spare moment to read a poem or a notice on the notice board. Make it a priority in your classroom.

Knowing texts

As a teacher of literacy it is imperative that you know about developments in texts. You need to know about children's authors and literature and you need to know about other forms of texts too. Make it your business to know what the children in your class are reading and watching, and read and watch it yourself. Know what texts you can recommend to them; as you get to know the children in your class and know their hobbies and interests, get to know books which you can recommend to them and which will develop them as readers.

Use expert knowledge

There are many resources out there to help you and you must take advantage of them as no teacher can expect to be familiar with everything. Below are just some of them:

Schools Library Association, www.sla.org.uk
United Kingdom Literacy Association, www.ukla.org
National Association for the Teaching of English, www.nate.org.uk
Books for Keeps, www.booksforkeeps.co.uk
Carousel Guide to Children's Books, www.carouselguide.co.uk

Book Trust, www.booktrust.org.uk
National Literacy Trust, www.literacytrust.org.uk

Talk

There is an abundance of evidence to show that talk is a key factor in the learning process and so it needs to be a central feature in literacy teaching. Do not feel pressurised into thinking that every lesson must have a written outcome but consider how you are going to monitor the learning. Early years practitioners are often recognisable because they carry around with them a notebook or pad of sticky notes and pencil with which they record not only the interesting things they see children doing but also the interesting things they hear children say. It would be good if every primary teacher emulated this practice.

However, an implication of this is that you create opportunities for all kinds of different talk. Use Alexander's (2008) characteristics of dialogic teaching to ensure that the opportunities you create are conducive to talk with the potential for learning:

- Collectivity – plan for you as the teacher and the children to address learning tasks together both as part of groups or in whole class circumstances. This will mean that you will create genuine problem-solving or enquiry-based lessons.
- Reciprocity – create an ethos within your classroom of teacher and children listening to each other, sharing ideas and learning to consider alternative viewpoints. Do not feel you need to give the impression that you are always correct.
- Cumulation – plan for opportunities which build on each other so that knowledge and understanding are created as teachers and children build on their own and others' ideas, chaining them into coherent lines of thinking and enquiry.
- Support – be sure that in your classroom children feel secure enough to express their ideas freely and without embarrassment.
- Purposefulness – identify clear and specific learning outcomes and make those apparent to the children.

You will see that all of these characteristics require the teacher to relinquish some control and this can be challenging. Do not be afraid of silence when children can think; allow children to think aloud and do so yourself, and make sure any question you ask opens up thinking and learning rather than closing it down.

Recognise the importance of talk and plan for it specifically. It is not just a few minutes on a plan labelled 'discussion' which you use to test knowledge or draw the class together.

Teaching reading and writing

Unsworth (2001) outlines three types of literacy learning and teaching which can be found in classrooms:

- Recognition is when children recognise and can reproduce the different codes that are used to construct and communicate meanings.
- Reproduction is when they understand and can produce different texts in appropriate ways and formats.
- Reflection is when they understand that texts are socially constructed and can stand back and reflect on the nature of texts and the implicit values and understandings contained in them.

How is this evident in what happens on a day-to-day basis? How do teachers plan to ensure that children not only recognise but can reproduce and reflect? I want to propose that these are not hierarchical or linear but that each type of literacy teaching and learning can take place in every classroom – a Foundation Stage 1 classroom and a Year 6 classroom. What does it look like?

In primary classrooms children are taught 'how to' read and write. They take part in shared reading and writing, guided reading and writing and independent reading and writing. They have daily discrete phonic teaching. Their environment is full of print used for genuine purposes and responded to. They are read to several times every day. What moves all those activities from the recognition to the reproduction and the reflection are the interactions that take place between the children and an informed teacher. While reading a notice the teacher will discuss who put the notice up and what message they want to convey; when sharing a book the teacher will encourage the children to relate what they read to their own experiences and evaluate its authenticity; when writing a letter the recipient will be considered and their perceived needs and understandings will determine what is put into the letter and how it is expressed.

Talk is the central element and it is what can change a mundane lesson instructing in skills to an exciting and powerful reflection on the use of literacy.

Literacy across the curriculum

I have a strongly held belief that literacy is at the heart of the curriculum and accept Langer's (1986) claim that it is a 'way of thinking'. This means that in every lesson teachers should be aware of the literacy demands that are being placed on children and plan accordingly. Whether you are teaching in a cross-subject way, a creative way or a subject-based way, children will need to use literacy in the lessons. Teachers need to ensure that they have the skills which are required.

This emphasises the fact that the first and most important thing a teacher must do when planning is to identify the learning objective, that is, you need to be absolutely clear in your own mind what it is you want children to gain from this lesson. If it is a history lesson and you want them either to learn that things were different in the past or what it felt like to be an evacuee in the Second World War, you need to be sure that nothing in the lesson will distract from that learning intention. For example if you ask them to read a text that is too challenging or to write in an unknown format all energies will be focused on that and the thing you wanted them to learn will fade into the background. You need always to be aware of literacy within every lesson.

It also means, however, that literacy learning can be a focus of a lesson and any content can be used. In the history lesson about evacuees you can use drama techniques, critically read accounts from different perspectives or look for emotive words and phrases within a text. This would make it a literacy lesson but with the bonus of developing knowledge about the history curriculum.

Planning and assessment

The role of a teacher is to ensure that every child in the class is learning. It is relatively easy to keep children busy and amused but if you have not made a difference to their understanding, knowledge or skills it is a waste of time. This means that teachers are continually monitoring the learning and adjusting their plans accordingly. We have seen in observations how plans were changed and modified to address the needs of the class, of groups and of individuals.

The observations have also shown how it is possible to over-plan. This is very difficult for an inexperienced teacher, especially when you are reminded of the importance of detailed planning at every opportunity during your training! There are several key points:

- Know what the purpose of a lesson or a unit of work is – what do you want to achieve at the end of this time of teaching?
- What do the children know now? What do they understand? What can they do? That is your starting point.
- How does understanding in the subject develop from the starting point to where I want to go? As teacher, I need to know what the next step is – it might be the next set of phonemes to teach, it might be a more challenging text to read, it might be challenging assumptions.
- What teaching strategies will help me to address this development? What degree of scaffolding do the children need – shared, guided or independent?
- How will I know if the children have reached my hoped-for end point? What will tell me that they know, understand or can do? What evidence can I look for and how will I look for it and record it?

What does effective teaching in literacy look like?

When discussing the stages of planning above, most trainees have wanted to know what good or outstanding teaching looks like. In the introduction to this book I compared effective teachers to a swan gliding over the water. They look beautiful; there is scarcely a ripple in the water and they are progressing purposefully towards their destination. Under the water, however, they are busy paddling without which nothing would happen. I hope that the chapters in this book have enabled you to look under the water and to begin to understand the nature of what lies beneath and enables effective literacy teaching to take place.

At the risk of mixing images, I often compare learning to teach with learning to drive. At first you are very aware of all the component actions required: you turn on the ignition, check the mirrors, let in the clutch, go into, hopefully, first gear, let out the clutch trying hard to recognise what is described as the 'bite' and then lurch off down the road. It all seemed so difficult and complex and, if you were like me, you wondered if you would ever be able to do it. However, as an experienced driver you probably now do all those things without even thinking about them and, if asked, would find it difficult to articulate all that is involved in safely driving a car.

Teaching is exactly the same. Experienced teachers do all those things under the surface which make life in the classroom smooth and purposeful but often do not consciously think about it or articulate why they are doing it. That makes life difficult for trainee teachers. They need to understand what is happening and why it is happening because learning to teach is not just about copying what you see. I hope this book has helped you to see and understand the paddling of the feet under the water and to know the questions you need to ask about what you see in classrooms.

Effective teaching of literacy

Hall and Harding (2003) did a review of the literature on effective literacy teaching. They attempted to identify key teaching strategies which were effective but found that this was not straightforward. Some key features which seemed to emerge from all the studies were:

- a balance of direct skills instruction and more contextually grounded literacy activities
- integration of literacy modes, and linking with other curricular areas
- pupil engagement, on-task behaviour and pupil self-regulation
- teaching style involving differentiated instruction (incorporating extensive use of scaffolding and coaching and careful and frequent monitoring of pupil progress)

- links with parents and local community.

Look back over all the observations in this book and you will see that these features were present in many, if not all, of them. There is no one way to teach literacy and anyone who tries to tell you otherwise is misguided. As professionals, teachers are continually making judgements about children and the appropriate next steps. Often these judgements are immediate and are based on a solid basis of subject knowledge for teaching. 'Effective teachers of literacy … are alert to children's progress and can step in and use the appropriate method to meet the child's instructional needs. The "effective" teacher uses an eclectic collection of methods …' (Hall and Harding, 2003: 3).

It is challenging for trainee teachers to make sense of this process and to come to a position where they are able to make those judgements and decisions themselves. The report goes on to say that it is through observation and reflection that trainees will gain the required experience.

> Students in training will not only need to be exposed to this wide and varied array of teaching practices but will also need experience in blending these practices in different ways for different children. They will also need opportunities to reflect on their own and others' practice in the light of the research base. Case study and exemplification material would be useful supports for teacher educators in promoting this learning and reflection. (Hall and Harding, 2003: 4)

This book aims to provide those exemplifications and to model the process of reflection which leads to deep learning.

Becoming a teacher

The process of teacher training is extremely demanding and stressful. Hobson and Malderez (2005) identified some key themes which are shared by all teacher trainees:

- The language and the terminology – teaching is as full of jargon as any other profession. Do not be afraid to challenge your tutors, mentors and teachers to explain to you what they mean when you cannot understand the language.
- Relationships – the relationship you have with your school-based mentor is crucial to your growth as a teacher. If there is a problem here you must talk with your tutor or the headteacher.
- Relevance – trainees often want to know 'how to do it' and become impatient with theory lectures. The distinction between the two is not as obvious as it may first seem. Becoming a teacher is all about making sense of what is going on in the classroom and to do this meaningfully a framework of established knowledge and understanding is needed. That framework is often what is called theory. The research found that those who had had

more experience in school prior to training appreciated the need for understanding the 'why' (theory) more.

- Emotions – Hobson and Malderez found that:

  the process of becoming a teacher is a highly emotional experience for most trainees. Many trainees use highly emotive language, such as excitement, love, panic, shock and overwhelmed to describe aspects of their early experiences as trainees, and many trainees refer to experiences which have boosted their confidence on the one hand, and undermined their confidence on the other. (2005: 139)

  It is comforting to know that you are not the only one who experiences vulnerability and varying degrees of confidence. I am feeling both those emotions as I prepare to send this manuscript to the publishers! In teaching, we are making ourselves vulnerable because teaching is, among other things, sharing ourselves with our pupils. It is as we grow in experience that our confidence also grows.

- Being a teacher – it is an exciting and challenging thing to be a teacher and it is significant that we always talk about *being* a teacher rather than *doing* teaching. One trainee I worked with wrote in his reflective journal about two-thirds of the way through his training, 'At last I am beginning to feel like a teacher rather than just behave like one'.

Being a teacher is also about being a learner and all that that involves – asking questions, taking risks and collaborating with others.

Being a teacher of literacy is even more exciting because it means entering different worlds with your pupils and creating different worlds with them; it means discovering the power of language and different means of communicating with all sorts of people for all sorts of reasons; it means giving children the opportunity to become effective citizens of the future and to share in and contribute to the development of humanity. The stakes are high but the rewards are great.

Further reading

Grigg, R. (2010) *Becoming an Outstanding Primary School Teacher.* Harlow: Pearson.

Pollard, A. (2008) *Reflective Teaching: Evidence-Informed Professional Practice.* 3rd edn. London: Continuum.

REFERENCES

Alexander, R. (2002) 'The curriculum in successful primary schools: a response', keynote address given to HMI invitation conference, 14 October 2002.

Alexander, R. (2004) 'The curriculum in successful primary schools: a response', keynote address given to the HMI Invitation Conference on the 2002 Ofsted report *The Curriculum in Successful Primary Schools*.

Alexander, R. (2008) *Towards Dialogic Teaching: Rethinking Classroom Talk*. 4th edn. Thirsk: Dialogos.

Andrews, R., Torgerson, C., Low, G. and McGuinn, N. (2009) 'Teaching argument writing to 7 to 14 year olds: an international review of the evidence of successful practice', *Cambridge Journal of Education*, 39(3): 291–310.

Baldwin, P. and Fleming, K. (2003) *Teaching Literacy Through Drama: Creative Approaches*. London: Routledge.

Barnes, J. (2011) *Cross-curricular Learning 3–14*. 3rd edn. London: Sage.

Barrett, L. (2010) 'Effective school libraries: evidence of impact on student achievement', *The School Librarian*, 58(3): 136–9.

Barrs, M. and Cork, V. (2002) *The Reader in the Writer*. London: Centre for Language in Primary Education (CLPE).

Bennett, N. and Desforges, C. (1984) *The Quality of Pupil Learning Experiences*. Psychology Press.

Black, P. and Wiliam, D. (1998) 'Inside the black box: raising standards through classroom assessment', *Phi Delta Kappan*, 80(2): 139–48.

Black, P., McCormick, R., James, M. and Pedder, D. (2006) 'Learning how to learn and assessment for learning: a theoretical inquiry', *Research Papers in Education*, 21(2): 119–32.

Booker, C. (2004) *The Seven Basic Plots*. London: Continuum.

Booth, D. (2006) *Reading Doesn't Matter Anymore ...: Shattering the Myths of Literacy*. Markham, Ontario: Pembroke.

Bruner, J. (1996) *The Culture of Education*. Cambridge, MA: Harvard University Press.

Bruner, J.S. (1966) *Toward a Theory of Instruction*. Cambridge, MA: Belknap.

Bruner, J.S. (2003) *Making Stories: Law, Literature, Life*. Cambridge, MA: Harvard: Harvard University Press.

Cambourne, B. (2000) 'Observing literacy learning in elementary classrooms: nine years of classroom anthropology', *The Reading Teacher*, 53(6): 512–15.

Chambers, A. (2011) *Tell Me (Children, Reading and Talk) with The Reading Environment*. Stroud: Thimble Press.

Clarke, S. (2008) *Active Learning Through Formative Assessment*. London: Hodder Education.

Corbett, P. (2008) *Book-Talk* http://nationalstrategies..standards.dcsf.gov.uk/node/154871

Corbett, P. (2008) *Talk for Writing*. Crown Copywright.

Craft, A. (1999) *Creativity across the Primary Curriculum: Framing and Developing Practice*. London: Routledge.

Cremin, T., Mottram, M., Bearne, E. and Goodwin, P. (2008) 'Exploring teachers' knowledge of children's literature', *Cambridge Journal of Education*, 38(4): 449–64.

Cremin, T. and Myhill, D. (2011) *Thinking Critically About Writing: Writers' Voices in the Classroom*. London: Routledge.

Daniel, K. (2011) *Storytelling Across the Primary Curriculum*. London: Routledge.

Dawes, L. (2001) 'Interthinking – the power of productive talk', in P. Goodwin (ed.), *The Articulate Classroom*. London: David Fulton.

Dawes, L., Mercer, N. and Wegerif, R. (2000) *Thinking Together: Activities for Teachers and Children at Key Stage 2*. Birmingham: Questions.

DCSF (2008) *Talk for Writing: Primary National Strategies*. London: HMSO.

DCSF (2009) *Primary School Curriculum Omnibus Survey: Top Line Findings Report*. London: HMSO.

DfE (2010) *The Importance of Teaching: Schools*, White Paper. London: DfE.

DfES (2007) *Letters and Sounds*. London: DfES.

Dombey, H. (2010) *Teaching Reading: What the Evidence Says*. Leicester: United Kingdom Literacy Association.

Dyson, A.H. (1993) *Social Worlds of Children Learning to Write in an Urban Primary School*. New York: Teachers College Press.

Ehri, L.C. (1995) 'Phases of development in learning to read words by sight', *Journal of Research in Reading*, 18(2): 116–25.

Eke, R. and Lee, J. (2009) *Using Talk Effectively in the Primary Classroom*. London: David Fulton.

Flynn, N. and Stainthorp, R. (2006) *The Learning and Teaching of Reading and Writing*. Oxford: Wiley Blackwell.

Galton, M. and Simon, B. (eds) (1980) *Progress and Performance in the Primary Classroom*. London: Routledge and Kegan Paul.

Ginnis, S. and Ginnis, P. (2006) *Covering the Curriculum with Stories: Six Cross-Curricular Projects that Teach Literacy and Thinking Through Dramatic Play*. Carmarthen: Crown House.

Goodman, K. (1992) 'Why whole language is today's agenda in education', *Language Arts*, 69: 354–63.

Goodwin, P. (ed.) (2001) *The Articulate Classroom: Talking and Learning in the Primary Classroom*. London: David Fulton.

Goodwin, P. (ed.) (2005) *Literacy Through Creativity*. London: David Fulton.

Goodwin, P. (ed.) (2008) *Understanding Children's Books: A Guide for Education Professionals.* London: Sage.

Goodwin, P. (2011) 'Creating young readers: teachers and librarians at work', in J. Court (ed.), *Reading to Succeed.* London: Facet.

Goodwin, P. and Perkins, M. (2009) *Reading Aloud in the Primary School.* Paper presented at UKLA Conference 'Changing Horizons', University of Greenwich.

Goodwin, P. and Perkins, M. (2010) *Teachers Choosing Books to Read Aloud in the Primary School.* Paper presented at UKLA Conference, University of Winchester.

Goouch, K. and Lambirth, A. (2008) *Understanding Phonics and the Teaching of Reading: Critical Perspectives.* Maidenhead: McGraw-Hill/Open University Press.

Goswami, U. (2006) 'The brain in the classroom? The state of the art', *Developmental Science*, 8, 467–9.

Goswami, U. (2008) 'Reading, complexity and the brain', *Literacy*, 42(2): 67–74.

Gough, P.B. and Tunmer, W.E. (1986) 'Decoding, reading and reading disability', *Remedial and Special Education*, 7(1): 6–10.

Gove, M. (2009) Interview in the *Daily Telegraph*, 3 August.

Graham, J. and Kelly, A. (2007) *Reading Under Control: Teaching Reading in the Primary School.* 3rd edn. London: David Fulton.

Grainger, T. (1997) *Traditional Storytelling.* Leamington Spa: Scholastic.

Graves, D.H. (1983) *Writing: Teachers and Children at Work.* Portsmouth, NH: Heinemann Educational.

Grigg, R. (2010) *Becoming an Outstanding Primary School Teacher.* Harlow: Pearson.

Grugeon, E. and Gardner, P. (2000) *The Art of Storytelling for Teachers and Pupils: Using Story to Develop Literacy in the Primary Classroom.* London: David Fulton.

Hall, K. and Harding, A. (2003) A systematic review of effective literacy teaching in the 4 to 14 age range of mainstream schooling', in *Research Evidence in Education Library.* London: EPPI-Centre, Social Science Research Unit, Institute of Education, University of London.

Halliday, M. (1993) 'Towards a language-based theory of learning', *Linguistics and Education*, 5: 93–116.

Halliday, M.A.K. (1976) *Language as Social Semiotic.* London: Arnold.

Hardy, B. (1977) 'Narrative as a primary act of mind', in M. Meek, A. Warlow and G. Barton (eds), *The Cool Web: Pattern of Children's Reading.* London: Bodley Head.

Harrison, C. (2010) *Interdisciplinary Perspectives on Learning to Read.* London: Taylor and Francis.

Heath, S.B. (1983) *Ways with Words.* Cambridge: Cambridge University Press.

Hobson, A.J., Malderez, A., (ed.), Kerr, K., Tracey, L., Pell, R.G., Tomlinson, P.D and Roper, T. (2005) *Becoming a Teacher: Student Teachers' Motives and Preconceptions, and Early School-based Experiences During Initial Teacher Training* (ITT), DfES Research Report No 673.

Jeffrey, B. (ed.) (2006) *Creative Learning Practices: European Experiences.* London: Tufnell Press.

Johnston, R. and Watson, J. (2007) *Teaching Synthetic Phonics.* Exeter: Learning Matters.

Joubert, M. (2001) 'The art of creative teaching', in A. Craft, B. Jeffrey and M. Leibling (eds), *Creativity in Education.* London: Continuum.

Laevers, F. (ed.) (1994) *The Leuven Involvement Scale for Young Children* (Manual and video). Experiential Education Series, No 1. Leuven: Centre for Experiential Education.

Langer, J.A. (1986) *Children Reading and Writing.* Norwood, NJ: Ablex.

Lockwood, M. (2008) *Promoting Reading for Pleasure in the Primary School.* London: Sage.

Marsh, J. (2003) 'Connections between literacy practices at home and in the nursery',

British Education Research Journal, 29(3): 369–82.

Marsh, J. and Millard, E. (2000) *Literacy and Popular Culture: Using Children's Culture in the Classroom.* London: Paul Chapman.

Maybin, J., Mercer, N. and Stierer, B. (1992) 'Scaffolding learning in the classroom', in K. Norman (ed.), *Thinking Voices: The Work of the National Oracy Project.* London: Hodder. pp. 186–95.

Medwell, J., Strand, S. and Wray, D. (2009) 'The links between handwriting and composing for Year 6 children', *Cambridge Journal of Education,* 39(3): 329–44.

Meek, M. (1988) *How Texts Teach What Readers Learn.* Stroud: Thimble Press.

Meek, M. (1991) *On Being Literate.* London: Bodley Head.

Mercer, N. (1995) *The Guided Construction of Knowledge: Talk Amongst Teachers and Learners.* Clevedon: Multilingual Matters.

Mercer, N., Hennessy, S. and Warwick, P. (2010) 'Using interactive whiteboards to orchestrate classroom dialogue', *Technology, Pedagogy and Education,* 19(2): 195–209.

Merchant, G. (2007) 'Writing the future in the digital age', *Literacy,* 41(3): 118–28.

Michener, J.A. (n.d.) BrainyQuote.com. Retrieved June 6, 2011, from BrainyQuote.com http://www.brainyquote.com/quotes/authors/j/james_a_michener.html

Moon, J.E. (2004) *A Handbook of Reflective and Experiential Learning: Theory and Practice.* Abingdon: RoutledgeFalmer.

Morris, M. and Smith, S. (2010) *Thirty-Three Ways to Help with Spelling: Supporting Children Who Struggle with Basic Skills.* London: Routledge.

Mroz, M., Smith, F. and Harding, F. (2000) 'The discourse of the literacy hour', *Cambridge Journal of Education,* 30(3): 379–90.

Mullen, R. and Wedwick, L. (2008) 'Avoiding the digital abyss: getting started in the classroom with YouTube, digital stories and blogs', *The Clearing House,* 82(2): 66–9.

Myhill, D. and Jones, S. (2010) 'How talk becomes text: investigating the concept of oral rehearsal in early years' classrooms', *British Journal of Educational Studies,* 57(3): 265–84.

Nystrand, M. (1997) *Open Dialogue: Understanding the Dynamics of Language and Learning in English Classrooms.* New York: Teachers College Press.

Ofsted (2002) *The Curriculum in Successful Primary Schools.* London: Ofsted.

Ofsted (2005) *English 2000–05: A Review of Inspection Survey.* London: Ofsted.

Ofsted (2010) *Reading by Six: How the Best Schools Do It.* London: Ofsted.

Pahl, K. and Roswell, J. (2005) *Literacy and Education: Understanding the New Literacy Studies in the Classroom.* London: Sage.

Pang, E.S., Muaka, A., Bernhardt, E.B. and Kamil, M. (2003) *Teaching Reading.* Geneva: International Academy of Education.

Paratore, J.R. and McCormack, R.L. (eds) (2007) *Classroom Literacy Assessment: Making Sense of What Students Know and Do.* New York: Guilford Press.

Pascal, C. and Bertram, A.D. (eds) (1997) *Effective Early Learning: Case Studies of Improvement.* London: Hodder and Stoughton.

Pentimonti, J.M. and Justice, L.M. (2010) 'Teachers' use of scaffolding strategies during read alouds in the preschool classroom', *Early Childhood Education Journal,* 37(4): 241–8.

Pollard, A. (2008) *Reflective Teaching: Evidence-Informed Professional Practice.* 3rd edn. London: Continuum.

Rose, J. (2006) *Independent Review of the Teaching of Early Reading.* Rose Review. London: DCSF.

Rose, J. (2009) *Independent Review of the Primary Curriculum; Final Report.* London: Crown Publications.

Rosen, H. (1984) *Stories and Meanings.* Sheffield: NATE.

Rosen, M. (2010) Foreword to Dombey, H. and colleagues in the United Kingdom Literacy Association, *Teaching Reading: What the Evidence Says*. Leicester: United Kingdom Literacy Association.

Schön, D. (1983) *The Reflective Practitioner: How Professionals Think in Action*. New York: Basic Books.

Sinclair, J. and Coulthard, M. (1975) Towards an Analysis of Discourse. Oxford: Oxford University Press.

Smith, V. (2008) 'Learning to be a reader: promoting good textual health', in P. Goodwin. (ed.), *Understanding Children's Books: A Guide for Education Professionals*. London: Sage.

Smith, F., Hardman, F., Wall, K. and Mroz, M. (2004) 'Interactive whole class teaching in the National Literacy and Numeracy Strategies', *British Educational Research Journal*, 30(3): 403–19.

Taeschner, T. (1991) *A Developmental Psycholinguistic Approach to Second Language Teaching*. Norwood, NJ: Ablex.

Unsworth, L. (2001) *Teaching Multiliteracies across the Curriculum*. Buckingham: Open University Press.

Vasquez, V. (2010) 'Critical literacy isn't just for books anymore', *The Reading Teacher*, 63(7): 614–16.

Verenikina, I. (2004) 'From theory to practice: what does the metaphor of scaffolding mean to educators today?' *Outlines: Critical Practice Studies*, no. 2.

Wells, G. (1999) *Dialogic Inquiry: Towards a Sociocultural Practice and Theory of Education*. Cambridge: Cambridge University Press.

Wood, D., Bruner, J. S. and Ross, G. (1976) 'The role of tutoring in problem solving', *Journal of Child Psychology and Psychiatry*, 17: 89–100.

Wray, D., Medwell, J., Fox, R. and Poulson, L. (2000) 'The teaching practices of effective teachers of literacy', *Educational Review*, 52(1): 75–84.

Wyse, D. and Styles, M. (2007) 'Synthetic phonics and the teaching of reading: the debate surrounding England's "Rose Report"', *Literacy*, 47(1): 35–42.

Wyse, D. and Torrance, H. (2009) 'The development and consequences of national curriculum assessment for primary education in England', *Educational Research*, 51(2): 213–28.

Children's books referred to

Browne, A. (1997) *The Tunnel*. London: Walker Books.

Browne, A. (2008) *Gorilla*. London: Walker Books.

Cannon, J. (1993) *Stellaluna*. Oxford: Harcourt Children's Books.

Cronin, D. (2003) *Click Clack Moo: Cows that Type*. London: Simon and Schuster.

Geraghty, P. (1995) *Over the Steamy Swamp*. London: Voyager Books.

Geraghty, P. (2010) *Solo*. London: Anderson.

Hunt, R. (2003) *Getting Up*. Oxford: Oxford University Press.

Lobel, A. (1983) *Fables*. Trophy Press.

Murphy, J. (2007) *Peace at Last*. London: Macmillan Children's Books.

Rosen, M. (1993) *We're Going on a Bear Hunt*. London: Walker Books.

Sheldon, D. and Blythe, G. (1993) *The Whale's Song*. London: Red Fox.

Waddell, M. (1994) *Owl Babies*. London: Walker Books.

Willems, M. (2004) *Don't Let the Pigeon Drive the Bus*. London: Walker Books.

INDEX